New Parents Are People Too

Notice: This book is not intended to replace recommendations or advice from physicians or other health care providers. If you suspect you have a medical problem, we urge you to seek medical attention from a competent health care provider.

All names used in this book have been changed to preserve privacy.

Published by People Too Unlimited
5828 NW 26th Court, Boca Raton, Florida, 33496

Distributed by Greenleaf Book Group LP

For ordering information or special discounts for bulk purchases, please contact Greenleaf Book Group LP at 4425 Mo Pac South, Suite 600, Longhorn Building, 3rd Floor, Austin, TX 78735, (512) 891-6100.

Page design and composition by Greenleaf Book Group LP
Cover design by Greenleaf Book Group LP

Publisher's Cataloging-In-Publication Data
(Prepared by The Donohue Group, Inc.)

Buchalter, Sharon Fried.
New parents are people too : 8 secrets to surviving parenthood as individuals and as a couple /Sharon Fried Buchalter.—1st ed.
p. ; cm.

ISBN-13: 978-0-9790930-0-5
ISBN-10: 0-9790930-0-7

1. Parenting—United States. 2. Parents—Attitudes—United States. 3. Child rearing—United States. I. Title.

HQ755.83 .B83 2007
649.1 2007929045

Printed in the United States of America on acid-free paper

12 11 10 09 08 07 10 9 8 7 6 5 4 3 2 1

First Edition

My children remind me that the love of a couple can develop into a beautiful life. In this busy world, children remind us to be more patient and to appreciate all of life's miracles. Through the eyes of my children, I learn life's most valuable lessons.

I dedicate this book to my loving family—my husband, David, my son, Daniel, and my daughter Rachael. I love you more than words can say.

—Dr. Fried/Mommy

Contents

Acknowledgments

I'd like to acknowledge my husband, David. Thank you for your understanding and patience when I was working all hours of the night to meet deadlines. Thank you for listening, for your encouragement and for your unconditional love.

To my son, Daniel: You are the sunshine of my life. You are wise beyond your years. You are my son, my friend and my teacher; and you always encourage me to help the world. I love you.

To my daughter, Rachael the Rascal: You always keep me on my toes and teach me the importance of having patience and flexibility, and thinking outside of the box. You are the apple of my eye. You are my best girlfriend and I look forward to many years of watching the excitement of the world through your eyes.

To my parents, Ruth and Louis Fried: Although you are no longer with me in physical body, I feel your presence every single day. Your words of wisdom stream through my mind like a river that helps my words flow. You are a channel for my life's work of helping others. You always believed in me and made me believe in myself. I love you and I miss you.

To my brother, Marty: You always brighten my day and remind me of Dad with your great sense of humor. I always look forward to our times together.

To Aunt Dorothy and Uncle Murray (Poppy): Thank you for being surrogate parents to me and surrogate grandparents to Daniel and Rachael. You are always there to lend a helping hand, to encourage me and to remind me to believe in myself. Thank you for the pride you show in me and my family.

To George and Corinne Buchalter: I'd like to thank you for helping to contribute to the foundation of my success. Your support is greatly appreciated and I am most grateful.

To my niece, Mandy: You are like a sister to me and you are always close to my heart. Thank you for your endless faith in me and for your continued support and friendship.

To Sheila, Leslie, Jay, Justin, and the rest of the crew at Greenleaf Book Group: Thank you for believing in my message and for helping it come to fruition. You are consummate professionals and I have enjoyed every minute of working with you all. A special thanks to Alan Grimes at Greenleaf Book Group for his unbelievable dedication, hard work, and numerous helpful conversations.

To my friend Sharon Cohen Peress: I'd like to thank you for always believing in the value of the work I do. Thank you for always reminding me of the importance of making a difference in the lives of parents and children all over the world. You're always there to lend a helping hand. Thank you for believing in me.

To Rifka Liberow, Rabbi Liberow and the Liberow family: Thank you for believing in my purpose and for being a part of my team. Rifka-thank you for always being there to help me with Rachael. Thank you for your continued support and help with everything I do. You are a great friend and confidante.

To Dalia: Thank you for your support, inspiration and daily words of wisdom. I am happy that you have come back into my life.

To my friend Gayle: You're brilliant. You're always there in a pinch to help me. I couldn't do half of what I do without your help. You're a very big part of my life and you always will be. I love you.

To my lifelong friends, Lisa, Beth and Sheila: Thank you for your endless support and friendship. You are all dear to my heart and always will be.

Above all, I'd like to thank G-d. Through His blessings, my life's mission is being realized. Thank you for the merit of allowing me to be a channel to help people all over the world.

Introduction

Being a new parent can be the most rewarding time of your life, but it can also be a completely overwhelming experience. Raising children is the most important job you will ever have, and it is one that comes without a training manual. This book is full of valuable information that will guide you through self-coaching strategies that will help you get to know yourself better as a person. It will also help you to grow and become the loving mate and parent that you've always wanted to be.

Most books and new parenting classes focus on the skills of infant feeding, care, bonding and health. Yet, the deeper truth of effective parenting is that it all begins with you as a couple. How you will parent your child extends from your heart, emotional balance, thinking and people-skills that you have developed for yourself and in your relationships.

You and your mate need to grow together and be clear about your new roles as parents. *New Parents Are People Too* provides a commonsense approach to planning, problem-solving, goal setting, and fulfilling this successful journey to becoming a confident and resilient person. It will provide you the opportunity to start this new time in your life together as mates and parents in a loving, caring way.

Presenting self-coaching strategies to parents is the foundation from extensive work from my private practice, my workshops and my seminars. Self-coaching is based upon the idea that each of us is responsible for our individual learning and growth, and, ultimately, our behavior, especially as parents. When you combine self-coaching and parenting skills, you arm yourself with the tools to understand your behavior and see how your actions affect your relationships. These methods of change encourage effective communication, self-esteem, problem solving, conflict resolution, positive thinking, stress management, and the building of resilience.

As you improve your individual skills, you will then be empowered to become a positive, action-oriented coach to yourself. You can assist your mate and yourself in becoming the parents you desire to become. You can manifest your goals as a team. That is the true victory this book will help you achieve.

In this book you will find some fun features along the way. Each chapter contains questions for your self-assessment, followed by coaching tips so you can put new understanding into action. At the end of each chapter, the coaching tips are listed on wallet-sized cards that you can cut from the appendix and carry with you. These wallet cards affirm your positive focus on growth. Each chapter also contains real-life stories which demonstrate examples that can be applied in a positive direction.

You will begin your journey with "Your Pyramid of Success," which I developed as a reminder for you of the steps you are taking to reach your full success potential.

Part One of this book focuses on your personal growth and that of your mate. I will give you the tools you need to stop unproductive behaviors and set goals to bring about positive changes to your behavior and enhance your relationships.

Part Two of this book helps you put your goals into action, showing you and your partner how to work as a team. As an individual, you will learn how a healthy sense of esteem and confidence helps you and the people you interact with everyday. As a team, you will work with your mate to define your parenting images and styles, sharpen communication skills, and develop strategies in solving problems and resolving conflicts.

In Part Three, you will focus on developing your skills as a team and focus on the type of lifestyle you desire to practice as new parents. I will show you how to become resilient and manage stressors by focusing on your health goals such as diet, exercise and relaxation. You will learn how to listen to your intuition and be flexible and open to change. Most important, you will be cultivating love and caring into your relationship as mates and eventually as new parents.

To get the most out of using this book, it will be helpful for you to have a journal to record your assessment results, new goals and action steps. Each chapter contains at least one assessment of values, perceptions or skills. Respond to the assessments as honestly as possible. The assessments are guides to help you review how you feel about certain issues, how you might handle a conflict, or they may empower you to anticipate and solve problems and plan with your mate for this new role in your life. When you practice stress management or effective communication skills, you will want to make notes about your progress. In the realm of self-coaching, you have to see your progress; it serves to motivate you. As you move through this book, visualize it as the roadmap of your journey to parenthood. Your journal contains the impressions along the way, the thoughts and fears as you see them come up, and the appreciation for how you and your partner are exploring and growing together. Your journal becomes your daily diary of goals and accomplishments.

I am confident that you will enjoy this journey of self-discovery that will help prepare you as a new parent. You are now ready to begin your journey. I will provide you with the confidence and the tools you need to be educated, empowered and enlightened as a new parent. Good luck and enjoy your journey to success as a new parent and an improved person.

Your Pyramid of Success

New Parents Are People Too will walk you through a successful life journey unlike any other. This book has come into your hands at the perfect time, as you and your mate are ready to start your wonderful new role as parents.

To start our journey, let's first review a distinctive approach that I have developed, which combines self-help and self-coaching skills. The steps, which I call "Your Pyramid of Success," will help you achieve the ultimate goal of being a successful person, mate, and parent.

As you read this book, you will feel educated and empowered on your journey. Envision yourself easily climbing each step to the top of the **Pyramid of Success**, which is illustrated for you below.

Step 1: Planning your success You will devise a plan to learn about yourself as an individual and learn how to become your own life coach, and how to use these skills in your relationship.

Step 2: Organizing a path to change You will discover innovative ways of doing things and develop positive patterns in your relationship to prepare you for your roles as a new parent.

Step 3: Putting your goals into observable measures You will document your goals by writing them down on paper. You will use observable measures, making you more likely to achieve them. By writing goals down, you are affirming your commitment to complete these goals in your relationship.

Step 4: Turning your goals into action When you determine realistic goals and write down ways to achieve them, you'll find ease in turning goals into realities. You start this work with each other, as mates, and also individually. You'll become your own life-long coach in mastering your life plans.

Step 5: Integrating social interaction skills You will discover 8 secrets of empowering skills which are crucial for your happiness and success as a person as well as a couple and a parent. These include a strong foundation in self-esteem, motivation, and learning the amazing effects of clear communication and effective conflict resolution. The chapters in Part Two help you cultivate these skills and bring you to a new level of self-realization and helps you build strong relationships.

In Part Three, the chapters include the secrets of being successful new parents. This will include skills in learning how to be caring, patient, flexible, intuitive and resilient. The skills contribute to fulfilling partnerships and a winning parenting team.

Step 6: Combining emotional and social health to promote success In this step, you will see how emotional, social and spiritual well-being helps you on your path towards personal and parenting success.

Step 7: Monitoring your behavior and how it affects you and those around you Through observation, I show you how to monitor your newly acquired behavior so that you have awareness of how it affects your life and the lives of those around you.

Step 8: Modifying your goals and behaviors During this step, you learn how to modify your goals or work towards new goals as your family grows based on the principles in the Pyramid of Success. This will help you achieve the ultimate goal of reaching your full success potential.

Step 9: Full success potential When you arrive at the summit of the Pyramid of Success, you will feel educated, enlightened and empowered to achieve your greatest happiness and success in life as a new parent.

PART ONE

DEVELOPING YOUR PROACTIVE GOALS

Planning, organizing, and documenting your goals

CHAPTER ONE

What Makes You Tick?

CHAPTER OBJECTIVES

- Learn what motivates you.
- Understand how coaching is based upon learning, reviewing, and taking action.
- Know the value of self-coaching.
- Explore how lack of confidence keeps one from achieving goals.
- Recognize five common forms of unproductive behavior and learn to change those into productive actions.

Mastery in work and in life is about committing yourself to being excellent in everything you do, no matter how small and no matter if no one is watching. Do you practice excellence in your most private moments?

—Robin S. Sharma

Striving for Excellence

What kind of parent do you hope to be? The way you live your life now and in the coming months will determine your ability to give your best to your new baby. Let's begin by discussing how to achieve excellence and success and why it is so important to you and your expanding family.

What separates people who are successful in life from those who are not? The biggest factor is the ability to channel and direct one's own personal energy or power. Successful people have a consistent, focused effort of achieving their goals and dreams. They know who they are and they go for the gold.

You know yourself better than anyone else. You know your values, strengths, challenges, dislikes, emotions, and dreams. You have the ability to map out your success plan. Self-coaching provides a structure for you to make the changes you desire for success; therefore, I will show you how to be your own life-coach.

Successful people understand how to harness and focus their abilities and how to follow a consistent plan. If their plan isn't working, they examine, assess, make changes, and try again! Mentoring yourself through the coaching process benefits you in the same way through planning, reviewing, and continuing to develop successful steps to achieve your dreams.

However, not everyone completes the tasks or the projects that they start. People often make goals such as starting a new exercise program, quitting watching television every night or keeping in better touch with a friend. It is important to follow through on your goals, but also be flexible and be willing to alter those goals as you go.

When your new baby arrives, it may seem as if nothing goes according to the plan. This is normal—having a baby changes everything. However, it is possible to stay focused and on track, but flexible at the same time. If you feel like the impulse to follow through with your goals is waning, this is the exact moment you should think about those very goals and realize why you made them in the first place. Perhaps you need to redefine them. For example, let's say you and your mate agreed before your baby was born that you wanted to raise your child in New York City. Perhaps you both find it difficult raising the baby in the city. Perhaps you want to move closer to your family. It's OK to redefine your goals and alter your plans. Sit down as a team and decide what is best for your family.

As a new parent, it is normal to feel tired. However, if you find yourself wanting to follow the path of least resistance, then take it as a challenge. Remember your goal of being the best parent you can be. Become your own best cheerleader and follow through on your commitment to success as an individual and a parent.

Coaching is based upon learning, reviewing and taking action. As you move through this book, you will discover things about yourself, review whether or not behaviors or patterns work for you, and make a choice for action. I will show you how to stick with what works for you and to change what doesn't. First, let's start by finding your motivating factors and what makes you tick.

What Makes You Tick?

A self-coaching program begins by identifying what motivates you. There are three main categories of motivation:

- What you feel is not right in your life: You have the impulse to change behaviors or situations that are telling you to "do something."

- Your desire to continue with and get more of what is right in your life: This can be money, love, personal accomplishments, artistic endeavors, etc.
- Your personal desire to grow and stretch beyond your comfort level: This motivates you to want to increase your effectiveness in your profession, personal relationships, finances, and health.

Exercise

Now I'd like you to review the three types of motivation for a self-coaching program. Write a brief letter to yourself about what makes you tick. Include answers to these three questions:

- What is not right in my life that I would like to change?
- What things are going right in my life that I want to increase and continue doing?
- In what areas of my life do I want to increase my effectiveness?

This exercise will help you learn where to focus your efforts. The more you learn about yourself, the more you will learn to value your special talents, express your ideas and gain confidence in areas of growth and opportunity.

Designing the Plan

Did you know that you can design and live the life of your dreams? You simply need a treasure map or planning guide for how to get there. I'm going to show you how to map your goals in order to live your best life and achieve your dreams.

When you cook a meal, you plan ahead by ensuring that you have all of the ingredients, as well as the time to prepare a delicious fare. If you plan a fund-raising event, you set goals for how much money you will raise, and then design a campaign to acquire the funds. Remember, successful new ventures always begin with a plan.

It is your time now to learn personal life-coaching skills for yourself that you can also use in your relationship with your mate, and when you have children. The next section will help you analyze who you are.

In Chapter Two, you will take this information and use it to help you make a personal plan for success.

At times, taking a hard look at yourself may not be easy; embracing change is a difficult task for most people. However, your task now is to enter the unfamiliar waters of change. I'm not asking you to dive in headfirst. I want you to get a feel for the water first, taking one step at a time according to your comfort levels. With practice and patience, you will learn to be your own successful life coach!

Self-Esteem

One of the most common feelings that people encounter when making changes is lack of confidence. One of the hardest facts you will face is the tendency to sabotage your own efforts for success. People often have unproductive habits that inhibit their personal growth by blocking the ability to make necessary changes for success. In addition to being willing to embrace change, you must build up your self-confidence and believe in your ability to make positive changes in your life.

Real-life Example

Jenna had gained quite a bit of weight and none of her clothes were fitting. She was two sizes larger than she normally was. Jenna had been planning to start a diet plan, but it did not happen. She was too busy, worked overtime, and took coaching classes for her job as a supervisor at a customer call center. There always seemed to be a reason not to diet.

What finally bolstered Jenna's confidence was a promotion at work, which was a wonderful surprise. Jenna's manager had seen her consistent effort and her desire to better herself, and admired her coaching skills at work. That boost to Jenna's self-confidence fueled her enthusiasm to push even harder for *all* of her goals. She became her own mentor and developed a plan for healthy eating. She joined a weight loss program and support group and lost weight the healthy way. Before long, Jenna loved her "new self."

Jenna's motivation for developing her personal success program came from her relationship with her manager, who believed in her.

Whether you find your motivation in relationships or within yourself, don't delay starting your self-coaching program. Do not ignore your old behavior patterns or obstruct your personal growth with excuses. Find a motivating force and take the first step. Exclaim: "Yes, I am willing to achieve my goals and live my dream!"

Reminders for Improvement

I am proud of you for taking the initiative to read this book and learn about yourself. This shows that you want to make positive changes and are ready to embrace change and plan the next phase of your life successfully! Your next challenge and responsibility is to assess your behaviors and determine if they are favorable or unfavorable to your personal relationships. The great news is that you can turn weaknesses into strengths, as long as you are willing to make the effort.

To help keep you focused, I have put together the following list of reminders and things you should be aware of when making improvements in your life:

- If you persist and work hard to alter negative or unproductive behaviors, you will eventually see the desired results. *Persistence is your key to success!*
- Choose to change one behavior at a time. In the next section, you will see different personality behaviors for you to review. Start small as to not overwhelm yourself if you find behaviors that you want to change. Once you have identified that behavior, you can then break that one behavior down into smaller steps, which should be relatively easy to achieve. Once you've mastered changing one behavior, you can be proud of your accomplishment and move onto the second behavior you'd like to change.
- Do not worry if you fall back a step or if old habits creep in. *A setback does not mean a relapse!* Continue on towards achieving your goal and making that change.
- Realize that the challenges you have experienced in your life have helped you develop skills and behaviors that got you where you

are today. Now you are refining your strengths and changing bad habits that no longer serve you. Be content with your past and be ready to embrace your future!

Now I'd like to review five common forms of unproductive behavior. As you read, see if you recognize any of these behaviors in your own life. Once you've reviewed each behavior pattern, I will discuss ways you can improve this negative behavior.

Behavior Pattern 1: The Intimidator

Characteristics of the Intimidator

Intimidators use their position of authority, size, intelligence, or talent to torment or put down other people. Intimidators like to flaunt themselves above others, usually trying to make themselves look good, achieve their goals, or to overpower another person. An intimidator may invade personal space by getting in someone's face or leaning into the conversation.

Intimidators are quick to criticize others; yet they provide little or no constructive solutions or suggestions. Another persecuting behavior that intimidators use is to laugh at someone or make them the butt of jokes. Intimidators put down others by using threats, alienation or withdrawal.

Intimidators feel a false sense of power that does not come from confidence and integrity, but rather from a sense of powerlessness. Intimidators have been programmed to feel unsafe, unsure, and powerless. Their feelings of power come from manipulation and overpowering others, most likely having been manipulated and overpowered themselves in the past. Intimidators may find themselves lonely. They may alienate people, causing friends to escape their intimidation.

Self-Analysis for an Intimidator

Are you an intimidator? Do you play this role in your work life or personal life? To think this through, I'd like you to ask yourself the following questions:

- *What am I gaining by acting this way? What is my payoff?*

Intimidators put others down because they want to feel bigger than others; they want to be someone other people will admire. They feel they deserve admiration because they are more intelligent, gifted, or more capable than their victim. Another factor that influences this type of action is fear. Fears that can run through an intimidator's mind are, "What if she can do the job better than I can?" or, "What if everyone likes him better than they like me, and I'm left out in the cold?" To avoid these situations, intimidators will do whatever they can to bring down the perceived offender and make sure everyone thinks she is better than the others.

- *Are the results of my behavior worth my feelings of alienation? Do I want people to avoid me, not invite me to social gatherings, and loathe being around me?*

An intimidator may experience a sense of inflated self-importance for a short time; however, when looking at the bigger picture, an intimidator is most likely not getting the results he wants and personal needs are not being met. People will often call an intimidator a bully behind his back, even though they might be nice to his face. An intimidator may win an occasional battle, but he will lose the overall war. People feel no empathy or compassion for an intimidator.

- *How would my life be better if I changed my behavior?*

Take a hard, honest look at the results of your life. Do you feel successful, or do you feel that you always have to prove yourself? Do you have friends? Are you happy with the social circle of people with whom you work or socialize? Are you always on the outskirts of a group? If you are not satisfied in these areas and you think it may be the result of playing the role of Intimidator, then try your best to change the negative behavior and turn your strengths into positives.

Making Positive Changes: Removing intimidating characteristics from our behavior

Making adjustments to an intimidating behavior pattern will help you be a better person. You will be able to surround yourself with people who want to be around you and whose company you enjoy. The following are some positive suggestions about modifying intimidating patterns:

- Give credit to other people. Appreciate the efforts of others who contribute to your project, household chores, or solutions. Do not slough off others' efforts or take credit for yourself.
- Rather than point out another person's mistakes, make an effort to find something positive to praise or for which to give them credit. Everyone makes mistakes. We are all vulnerable to human error.
- Listen to, consider, and, if feasible, use an idea proposed by someone else. Be open to new ideas. This will not only increase the morale of other people, but will also expand your knowledge base. Most people are more likely to work *with* another than *for* another. The result will be better productivity on the job and possibly friends or social acquaintances.

Inspiration: Use the power that makes you intimidating to instruct and to help. Become a friend or leader that people look up to and want to emulate.

Behavior Pattern 2: The Doubter

Characteristics of the Doubter

The doubter is unsure of his abilities and will consistently do everything by the book and by the rules. The doubter will do what is already proven to work in order not to make mistakes. She lives with her perceived inadequacies and projects those feelings of insecurity onto other people. A doubter demonstrates rigid behavior and rarely engages in few creative or inventive activities. Socially, the doubter is excluded from activities in favor of others who are less afraid of new situations and who are more adventurous. A doubter may go out of her way to not participate in activities or jobs that stretch her too far or make her feel uncomfortable.

Self-Analysis for the Doubter

Do you fall into the category of a doubter? Do you find that some of the doubter descriptions fit you? To think this through, I'd like you to ask yourself the following questions:

- *Did you once try a new idea that failed?*

If this has happened to you, just remember that you are not alone. Remember and learn from the words of Thomas Edison who stated, "No experiment is a failure." You may have been disappointed and emotionally hurt, but think about what you learned from your effort. Think of a time when you made a mistake, and then see the gift of your effort. What did you learn that would help you be more resilient or insightful? One success out of 200 is better than zero successes out of zero.

- *Has a former friend or mate influenced you by not giving you the option of trying new ideas?*

Think of how the growth of your creative output might have been stunted. Is this what you want to pass on to others? By allowing those close to you to see their ideas pass or fail, you are giving them the opportunity to learn for themselves and to spark creative growth. By encouraging an exchange of ideas and being receptive to the plans of others, you are entering into a win-win situation.

- *Hae friends laughed at you for not being very skilled when something out of the ordinary was attempted?*

Not everyone can be a talented artist, mountain climber, accomplished dancer, or Olympic swimmer. No one can excel at all things. Instead of feeling inadequate, one defense is to develop a good sense of humor. Another approach is to find your talent and nurture it. Give your life a personal purpose and pursue it passionately.

- *What would be the worst-case scenario for a failed idea?*

Would you be fired from your job? Not likely. Instead, you would probably be encouraged to re-work the plan to make it feasible. Would you be laughed at? No. It is more likely that you would be praised for having the idea in the first place and for putting it into action, even if it did not work out. Would your friends make fun of you for not being skilled at an activity or for not participating if the idea fails to interest you? No. They would appreciate your sense of humor and your honesty. They might even ask you to suggest the next group activity so that you can participate and enjoy it.

Making Positive Changes: Removing doubt from our behavior

The following are some positive suggestions for how you can modify your doubting behavior.

- Discover why you may be lacking confidence. To become more self-confident, break out of your routine and do one thing different each day for one week. Make some small changes and gradually move on to bigger changes as your confidence grows. For example, when your mate notices your receptiveness, he will be more open to support you and participate in new endeavors. Friends will be more likely to call on you when they discover your new attitude about participating in diverse activities.
- What you can always do is try your best and accept that some of your ideas will not turn out as you expected. Then, try to improve upon those ideas. Remember, it is impossible to be all things to all people.

Inspiration: Once you start to build your confidence and self-esteem, you can readily relate to those who face similar challenges. Use your new understanding to build bridges and strengthen relationships.

Behavior Pattern 3: The Skeptic

Characteristics of the Skeptic

The skeptic is a person who distrusts ideas that are not his own. A skeptic belittles others' plans and suggestions for no reason other than distrust. While it can be healthy for people to question ideas and suggestions so that they can accept them in their own mind, skeptics delight in consistently rejecting other people's proposals. A skeptic manages to undermine others' self-confidence through criticism, constant questioning or badgering remarks. Constant ridicule, especially from a mate or parent, is extremely destructive and can easily put a halt to creativity.

Self-Analysis for the Skeptic

If you feel that you play the role of skeptic or fall into this category, I would like you to reflect on the following questions to determine how you can alter your behavior.

- *Do you give your full attention to others?*

Consider how you have responded over the past two months to ideas that were expressed by your mate or your friends. Were you critical before hearing what they had to say? Was your mind closed? In order to change your behavior, you must give your mate or friend your undivided attention and listen. This means listening without judgment or interrupting to comment with your opinion, unless you're specifically asked to do so. When you really focus on their comment and do not divert your attention, you will discover interesting and important things that may influence your own thinking.

- *Can you honestly say that you give consideration to others' ideas?*

When you enter a conversation with your mate, do you always need to be right? Do you bring preconceived notions or negativity to dialogues with friends? By doing this, you are not giving shared discussions the contemplation they deserve. The skeptic can look egotistical because he only trusts his own ideas. Usually he has the experience to support his ideas. At the same time, the skeptic has a difficult time believing that anyone else could have a better solution.

- *Do your comments cause a group alive with conversation to suddenly become silent?*

Closed-minded skepticism can stop creativity cold. The skeptic has a very difficult time delegating to others. Thus, the skeptic is usually not a good team player.

- *If another idea is accepted over yours, do you feel it will undermine your authority?*

Watch carefully how a leader delegates authority and asks for plans and assistance. You will discover that the majority of workable plans do not come from the person in charge, but from the people who work with or under the leader. Does this diminish a leader's authority? Not at all. As a matter of fact, the leader receives praise for having good teammates who are motivated and successful. This makes the leader look even better.

- *Does listening to others make you less of a leader?*

The skeptics often alienate the people they love or admire the most because of an inflated belief in their experiences. No one, no matter what his position in life, can do it alone. Be willing to ask for help, new ideas and support.

Making Positive Changes: Removing skepticism from our behavior

I would like you to reflect on the following questions to determine how you can alter your behavior. The following are helpful suggestions for modifying and removing skepticism from your behavior:

- As hard as it may be, realize how comments affect others before you speak. Negative comments can curb enthusiasm. The absolute need to prove your point can kill creativity and cause others to not want to be in your company. In order to avoid this, stop yourself before making any negative comments.
- Be a good listener and be receptive to others' ideas and creativity.
- If you have a comment or suggestion to make, preface it with a positive statement first. For example, if your spouse cooks a beautiful dinner, but the potatoes are too spicy, start with a positive comment like, "The meal was delicious, but next time, maybe you can put less spice in the potatoes." You are still being positive, and you are also providing constructive feedback.

Inspiration: Skepticism can be the catalyst for rethinking a plan with possible flaws. When offering suggestions, remember that constructive criticism reflects intelligence; destructive criticism reflects a desire to control.

Behavior Pattern 4: The Perfectionist/The Hypercritical

Characteristics of the Hypercritical Person/Perfectionist

Perfectionists can be obsessive and inflexible about how to accomplish tasks. Perfectionists feel that they must always do everything best. For example, a homemaker might complain about the amount of work she has to do and the small amount of time available to accomplish all of the cleaning, cooking, and managing that is part of running a household. However, this same homemaker could eliminate much of the work by delegating it to other family members. The problem is that if this person is a perfectionist, she probably will not do this because she thinks that no one else can do the job as well as she can.

Perfectionists might not delegate responsibility to others. This can burden them with unnecessary anxiety and stress, which can compromise their health. By not entrusting tasks to other people, perfectionists deprive themselves of learning experiences. Others do not have the opportunity to learn from them either.

People who are hypercritical demand perfection not only in themselves, but also in others. They attack others' efforts in a way that promotes fear and self-doubt. If you fall into this category—beware. Nothing can turn a friend into a foe faster than a constant barrage of critical remarks.

An example of hypercritical behavior lies in the following example: A husband surprised his wife one evening by arriving home early, fixing a gourmet dinner, and serving her wine with her meal. They enjoyed a lovely dinner and dessert together. He topped off the evening by cleaning up the kitchen and loading the dishes into the dishwasher. The hypercritical wife inspected the dishwasher and proceeded to rearrange the dishes and instruct him on how to properly load the machine. By being so hypercritical and focusing on the negative rather than the positive, the hypercritical wife could easily have caused her husband not to want to do nice things for her anymore, in fear of rejection.

Self-analysis for the perfectionist/hypercritical

- *As a child, were you always expected to be perfect?*

Some parents expect their children to be perfect, which is just not realistic. Human beings learn from their mistakes. Children who are bullied into perfection cannot make the mistakes they need in order to learn. By the time these children grow into adults, they often abhor errors in themselves and in others. They set personal or professional goals that they can rarely attain.

- *What would happen if you failed to show perfection?*

Would you be fired? No. Would your family suffer? No. Would your friends wonder what happened to you? They might, but it would be from a positive concern. People around you would learn to relax and not always be on guard, trying to do everything as well as you. As a result, there would be a lot more smiles when you were around.

- *Do you feel like your world would fall apart if you made a mistake?*

Look around and you will see that people make mistakes every day; yet the world still exists. By understanding that everyone makes mistakes, you will alleviate much of the pressure you are under and will feel better physically and mentally.

Making Positive Changes: Removing hypercritical characteristics from our behavior

The following are some suggestions for how you can modify perfectionist or hypercritical tendencies and behavior.

- Recognize that attention to detail can be an asset in some situations, and no one else may have your eye for detail. If you can learn to accept an 80% level of perfection, life will be much easier for you and everyone around you.

- Begin to accept some amount of imperfection, one small step at a time. How do you do this? Allow your mate to do the dishes while you remain in another part of the house. Do not make negative comments about the job. Instead, show appreciation for her efforts.
- Relax and take a deep breath. Change your perception and stop seeing errors in others. Look for their positive qualities and show appreciation for their efforts. Learn to see the funny side of a mistake. Humor is a wonderful way to show that you, too, are human. If you relax, others will feel more relaxed around you.

Inspiration: Always be more willing to delegate behavior and remove the workload from your shoulders.

Behavior Pattern 5: The Loner

Characteristics of the Loner

Loners are usually very intelligent people who work well on their own. This positive trait helps them focus on and accomplish their goals. On the down side, loners are usually not good team players. They may have problems communicating well-thought-out plans to others.

Loners can appear to be distant and uninterested. There are times, however, when even loners crave company. They need someone with whom they can celebrate victories and commiserate losses.

Loners may be uncomfortable in group situations. In a partnership such as marriage, loners may prefer time alone, involved in solitary activities. If they don't communicate their needs to their mate, misunderstandings can cause communication problems and hurt feelings. In social situations, loners are unwilling participants in group activities and are often wrongly perceived to be standoffish when, in fact, they are actually just uncomfortable.

Self-Analysis for the Loner

If you feel that you play the role of Loner, ask yourself the following questions:

- *Have I always felt this way? If not, when did I start feeling this way?*

In some individuals, the preference for being alone starts in childhood. Perhaps you were brought up as an only child and often had no one else to play with. Perhaps you became accustomed to playing alone and, eventually, felt uncomfortable in a group setting. These feelings may have carried over into adulthood and become a habitual way of life.

Even if you were not an only child, you may still have developed problems with communication and interactions. Your preferences may have set you apart and left you out of the loop.

Children who are loners feel pulled between the desire for friendships and quiet time, to be part of the group *and* enjoy your own solitude. At some point, you may have given up on the group and settled for your own company.

- *Do I feel superior to others? Inferior to others?*

Someone who has feelings of superiority feels like she is better than others. Others may choose not to associate with her. People sense a superior attitude and avoid unnecessary interaction with that person. The opposite of superiority is inferiority. Inferiority can also set you apart from others. Feelings of inferiority could make you think, "They don't want me around. I'm not as intelligent (athletic, friendly, fashion conscious, etc.) as they are. I won't give them the chance to shun me. I'll just stay by myself."

Making Positive Changes: Removing loner characteristics from our behavior

The following are some suggestions for how you can modify loner behavior:

Socially, there are several ways to modify your loner behavior:

- Learn to spend more time with others. You may not be the life of the party, but you can increase your interaction with others.
- Work to cultivate one or two close friends. Through these friends, you will be drawn into a circle of acquaintances with whom you can feel comfortable.

- Be selective in the social invitations you accept, but make a serious effort to spend time in the company of others on a regular basis.

Personally, there are several ways to modify your loner behavior.

- Make every effort to communicate to your mate what your reasons are for needing to be alone. Explain that quiet time is about you and has nothing to do with him. Ask your mate not to take it personally. Encourage your mate's personal interests and desires to sometimes be alone.
- If the opportunity for interaction is possible, then invite your mate to join you, even if each of you is involved in quiet, separate activities.
- Plan an evening alone with your spouse, in which your attention is on him.

Your Personal Assessment

The five personality types above might reveal glimpses into some possible behaviors and interactions in your own life. Learning about behavior types helps you understand how you can achieve your success plan and what struggles you may endure. If you need to improve your communication skills, then this learning will be part of your success plan.

Do you need to improve your social skills? How will you plan to do this? How can you capitalize on your strengths and grow into competencies? How you perceive yourself is the foundation of your self-coaching program. To be aware of which of your behaviors can achieve results, you must know *who* you are and be comfortable with that. You must have great courage to analyze which behaviors do not achieve results; and you must be willing to change those behaviors and replace them with positive behaviors.

How you perceive yourself in relationships has significant impact on your success plan. Others will feel your emotions and relate to your social skills. In partnership, business, or friendship, behavioral guidelines will empower you to stretch beyond your comfort zone in order to build a loving, supportive network in your life.

Summary

In this chapter, you learned the value of a self-coaching program for preparing yourself for success. First you identified motivating factors in your life, and how those factors affect a person's ability to take positive action. You learned to recognize five common forms of unproductive behavior and how to change those into productive actions.

In the next chapter, you will take this information and start the first aspect of your personal plan for success.

Wallet Card

Below, you will find some simple coaching points to remember. For each chapter, a corresponding wallet card is provided for you in the appendix. Read the points from the end of each chapter, then cut each card out from the back of the book and keep it with you to remind you of your goals.

- I have consistent, focused effort.
- I am my best cheerleader & motivator.
- I always follow through for success.
- I change one behavior at a time.

CHAPTER TWO

Bringing Your Plan to Life!

CHAPTER OBJECTIVES

- Know yourself better by exploring values.
- Through honest responses, determine the challenges in your values or behavior that you will change.
- Prioritize areas of growth.
- Make a plan for changes, one step at a time.

> Knowing others is intelligence; knowing yourself is true wisdom.
> Mastering others is strength; mastering yourself is true power.
>
> **—Lao-Tzu**

Know Yourself Well

Great things happen to good people who can follow their road maps to success. Achieving one's plan for success usually is not a problem unless your choices appear confusing. If you are unsure of your choices or a direction is not clear, then it is time to review your values and the goals of your success plan to insure that they still serve you.

For example, Karen is a school counselor who deals with children's emotional ups-and-downs five days a week. She knows that when she leaves the school building at 5 PM each day, she should leave her concern for her students behind her. Her evenings are usually filled with doctoral coursework two nights a week and studying another two nights a week. Friday night is Karen's night to take it easy, a time when she lounges and watches a favorite movie while cuddling with her cat.

Karen has established this planned time for her personal renewal. Yet, she has a hard time saying no; so now and then she gives her phone number to a parent who "might" need to call her. Sure enough, when a parent calls Karen for counseling advice, an hour of her precisely-timed evening of renewal is gone. Once a parent called and Karen missed her evening class.

The dilemma that Karen faces is clear. On the one hand, she cares for her students and their parents and wants to assist them. On the other, she must have time for her studies if she is to complete her doctorate, as well as her renewal evening if she is to maintain her health. She is tightly scheduled for five days a week, and there is no room for deviation from her schedule. Karen's caring availability and her other structured time demands clash with each other. Being pulled from different directions causes her incredible stress.

As her own life coach, Karen reviews the situation and reprioritizes her success plan. She sticks with her tight schedule for five days. She considered giving her students' parents her phone number and taking calls on Saturday, which is her play day. She concludes that her play day is important for her mental health as she addresses students' needs five days a week. Karen dedicates her working hours to the students and parents that she serves, and recognizes that the rest of the week must be spent on study and rest in order for her to be satisfied and happy.

Knowing about yourself is helpful. Applying this knowledge you have about yourself is wisdom. Chapter one provided information for you to analyze regarding your temperament. This chapter provides further questions for your personal review and insight.

Moods and Behaviors

Below, you will find ten statements to complete by writing them out in your journal. When you are finished, review your personal profile for the areas in which you would like to grow. Then incorporate these into your plan at the end of the chapter. Because you and your mate have different ways of relating to the world and different characteristics, the assessment should be completed separately.

Exercise

Complete the following statements before reading further.

1. I am happiest when . . .
2. I get angry when . . .
3. I wish for . . .
4. What helps me through the hard times is . . .
5. I feel good about myself when . . .
6. I hate it when . . .
7. My worst fear is . . .
8. My spouse/mate treats me . . .
9. I love it when . . .
10. As a child, I was treated . . .

Explanations of each statement for your review

Statement 1: I am happiest when . . .

People define happiness in different ways according to what it means to them personally. What makes you happy? Are you an outdoor person who loves to hike and be in nature? Do you love the water and sunbathing at the beach? Perhaps your favorite activity is to build a warm fire in the fireplace and read a good book. Do you enjoy volunteer activities where you are in service to people? Perhaps you love the thrill of physical achievement like running a marathon or the challenge of sailing in windy waters. Do you like to work with team members or do you concentrate better when you are alone?

When you determine the activities that make you happy, I strongly suggest that you bring them into your life as you are able to manage the time and the activity. For example, if you crave the company of people to make your day more enjoyable, then consider including that in your work schedule and adding social gatherings and time with others and your spouse into your monthly calendar. Even men and women who work at home can schedule time out during the week for their interests: social lunches, book reading clubs, writing groups, or play dates in order to develop strong support networks. For the true networkers, this social strength adds to their happiness factor.

The happiness factor becomes especially important when planning a new family. Your friends and family will form part of your social support team. Scheduling time alone to sleep or renew your energy is equally as important as planning mate time. By deciding exactly what it is that makes you happier, you can determine how to spend your time and how you will focus your energy. Being happy and fulfilled puts you in charge of your life, and you are the only one who can make it happen. If you want it, then go for it.

Statement 2: I get angry when . . .

When examining anger patterns, it is good to distinguish between what triggers the petty annoyances and what can set off the bigger conflicts that may anger you. The little triggers can be as simple as having too much coffee to not getting enough rest. Small annoyances can be around work, time or people in your environment. Are there certain conditions at work that you can change or people that you need to speak with about ineffective behaviors? These underlying causes can be exacerbated through stress, lack of exercise, or hormonal changes.

If anger seems to be a chronic condition, then your life is out of balance. Like the Tower of Pisa, you may be leaning too far in one direction and feeling like you are not grounded and focused. The first place to examine for the root cause of chronic anger is your physical health. When you do not feel well physically, you may not have much patience with anything or anyone.

The second place to look for causes is within your primary relationships. Are you dissatisfied with some aspect of your marriage or arrangement? Are there words or feelings that you need to communicate to your mate, boss, parent or coworker? Are you having difficulty with managing time? I strongly suggest that you note these issues in your journal to include in your self-coaching plan.

Correct whatever seems out of balance in your life and determine if this lowers your levels of anger or chronic agitation. If you cannot control your anger, then seriously consider an anger management course so that your lack of control does not affect your relationships adversely for the rest of your life. Take positive action in your own behalf! You are worth the effort! Do not let a pattern of annoyance or anger undermine your good nature and all that you have accomplished.

Statement 3: I wish for . . .

Once in a while, I ask my clients what they would ask for if they only had one wish. Whether they respond with wishes for money, health, world peace or the perfect mate, I gain insight as to their values and their desires. What would you wish for if I asked you?

Would you wish for money? All of us need money for the proper care and feeding of ourselves and our families. Most of us also desire money for vacations and luxury items. Often the lack of money can lead to frustration, anger, and depression. If you feel that you need to have more money to properly care for yourself and to invest, know that the real world of money requires a real-world sensible approach and plan. Here are some self-coaching tips to get started:

1. List your personal needs and the needs of your partner and household on a monthly basis.
2. List the income from all sources and determine if your needs require more income than your bring in. If so, then list how you can cut back in the household expenses until you have some discretionary income after all monthly expenses are paid.
3. If you need more money, make a list of ways you could access more money and how you will do that.
4. Look at your supportive financial infrastructure. Do you need and have health insurance, life insurance, car insurance, etc.? Do you have any savings? Do you have a back-up plan for support if you were to get sick or fired tomorrow?
5. If a part of your financial infrastructure is missing, make a list of what you need to add to your list and how to achieve it.

So relax, put on your thinking cap and make a plan. You will feel more secure and comfortable when you know that your finances are under control.

If you wished for good health, there is plenty you can do to maintain a bright attitude and high vitality. The first thing you need to do is visit your doctor for a complete checkup. If your medical practitioner gives you a clean bill of health, then these are your basic health needs:

1. Physical health needs include sunshine, nutritional food, vitamins, minerals, and amino acids, and basic movement in some form of exercise.
2. Mental/emotional health needs usually revolve around stress management (see Chapter 9), keeping your mind stimulated through reading and creative expression and adding activities to your life that bring you pleasure, calm, and balance.
3. Spiritual health involves staying inspired and positive. Whether you belong to a community of people who share your religion or

you find inspiration in nature, relationships, prayer or meditation, living with purpose provides spiritual nourishment.

Make notes about where you feel you need growth in your journal now. Write goals in your individual plan at the end of this chapter. In just a short period of time, you will notice a difference in how you look and feel. Perhaps your mate will join you in cooking healthful meals or starting a new exercise routine. Both of you will look and feel better, and you will have done this in partnership. Moreover, you'll be preparing your health regimen to develop stamina and energy as new parents.

Statement 4: What helps me through hard times is . . .

How do you handle adversity? Do you think of yourself as a resilient person? If you do not have a favorite method to reduce stress and ease frustration when the going gets rough, you can become irritable. Your agitation rubs off on your mate and friends. If you currently have nothing in place to help you through adversity and build resilience (see Chapter Ten), try these suggestions.

Tell yourself, "I am safe. I can handle this. I will do it." Positively affirming your safety works, even if you are truly frightened or feel helpless. Speaking to yourself out loud works even better. In 1984, a friend of mine was hiking down a steep mountain goat trail in Peru when cold drizzle started falling. The rocky trail became slippery, and, of course, there were few handholds. Fear gripped her gut so that she couldn't take a deep breath. She started speaking to herself, "You can do it. Put one foot carefully in front of the other, and look at your feet. Place them carefully, one foot in front of the other. Slowly and deliberately, you are doing fine." So the conversation continued for four grueling miles down the trails. Flat ground never felt so good to her, and she was astonished at how focused she could be through positive self-talk.

Find your sense of humor, and laugh aloud if you have to. Go ahead and actually smile, which does bring a biochemical change for the better. This is not always easy to do, but, if you can manage it, you may see the problem as less overwhelming.

Statement 5: I feel good about myself when . . .

Think about a specific time when you really felt great about yourself, and burn the image into your memory. Add a smiling face, sparkling eyes, and a lively posture. When you are feeling blue, depressed, or generally moody, reach into your memory bank and think about the time that you felt fantastic or when you laughed so hard that you cried. Remember that moment. Feel that moment. Recapture it in your mind. Thinking about such images can make you a happier person, especially when you feel down.

Statement 6: I hate it when . . .

What are your pet peeves, things or situations that you say you hate? When what you hate is in your face, how do you handle it? How do you manage the small, disruptive situations without making enemies?

If you are being interrupted, kindly define your boundaries and explain what you must finish. Honest communication is always best, yet be thoroughly prepared so you will not stumble over your words when you discuss a delicate point. Know what you want to say. (See Chapter Seven on communication tips).

Always be honest. People respect honesty, even if they may not always like what you have to say. Being up front about your feelings will make people aware of them, and most people will be sensitive to them. I have found that people always prefer that a friend be honest than pull away and say nothing for fear of hurting feelings.

Statement 7: My worst fear is . . .

Whatever is your worst fear, the simplest formula for reducing fears and facing fearful situations is a three-step process:

1. *Awareness*: Pay attention or be aware of where you are holding fear in your body. Write down or speak to someone about the exact fear tapes that are running in your mind. Awareness of your fear means you are no longer in denial of it.
2. *Acknowledgment*: Speaking a statement about the fear or writing it in your journal helps you face your fear head on. When you see or

hear it directly, the intensity of the fear is reduced, and the fear no longer lurks in your head whispering to you about how much you are frightened. You have moved your fear from your inside to the outside, making it concrete.

3. *Acceptance*: Being aware of your fear and acknowledging your fear may be enough for the fear to diminish in its intensity or its ability to influence your life. This final step of acceptance opens the door for you to make a conscious choice about fear. Do you need it or want it, or can you banish it and focus on an affirming action?

For example, the wife of one of my clients hates roller coaster rides after a frightening incident as a child. Her husband convinced her to go again when they and their two children attended a carnival. As she stepped into the roller coaster car, she became nauseated, but was determined to stick it out. She closed her eyes and screamed her way through the ride. When she stood on solid ground again, her husband noted that she was wet with perspiration and got her a cold drink. She could not hold it down, and in front of carnival goers she vomited the soft drink. Was the ride worth getting over her fear? No! She accepted her fear just fine, informed her family that the upset to her balance and equilibrium was not worth it, and she went to sit down.

My client's wife didn't have any judgments about her fear as being good or bad. She accepted it as part of herself and chose not to ride a roller coaster again, ever. So when would you make changing fears a goal in your self-coaching plan? If you found that fears truly got in the way of your success, dream or life purpose, then you would develop a gradual plan for fear reduction and management. For example, if you desire to be a public speaker, did you know that the majority of people are afraid to speak in front of others? You are not alone, and even the best public speakers will admit to having butterflies before they get on stage. To de-sensitize your fears about public speaking, you develop a one-step-at-a-time approach to moving forward. Start with small, local groups and move to larger groups as you gain confidence.

First, you must realize that when you face an unknown, the mind conjures fears, illogical thoughts that cause you stress. To alleviate fears, you have to get information and make a plan. When you prepare yourself and arm yourself with all the data, education, tips, and news about the situation, you'll have an arsenal of tools to give you strength. Your mind will have the answers when your fear whispers, "What should I do?"

Create a safety net of friends or family members who agree to help, take your calls, or listen to your tears when needed. If you know that someone has your back, you will feel safer to have new experiences. Your friends, if they are true friends, will be happy for your success and happy to help stabilize the fears.

Another secret is time management. Learn how to manage your time, and you will conquer even more than you thought you could handle.

Statement 8: My spouse/mate treats me . . .

If your spouse treats you like a child, perhaps it is because—to an extent—you not only reinforce, but even expect that type of behavior. Consider your interactions with her and commit to make a behavioral change. Do you pout? Do you throw a tantrum? Do you charm your mate into agreeing with you? If this behavior reminds you of a child, then remember the adage, "If you're going to act like a child, then you'll be treated like a child."

However you perceive that your spouse treats you, consider how you might have enabled it. Do you feel you are treated as inferior? This stems from your low self-esteem. Examine how you feel less than others. Do you feel unappreciated? Examine how you disregard your gifts or values. Use the following steps to clarify your behavior and examine your values and goals.

In future interactions and situations, keep the inferior or childish responses out of your interactions. Speak calmly and make your points clearly. Discuss your differences like adults.

If you feel treated like a child, then understand that by acting as an adult, you may not always get your way. You may end up in compromise or even disagreement. You can agree to disagree, and you will have earned your mate's respect by acting like an adult.

If you are feeling that you are treated as inferior, then recognize your own talents and refuse to allow yourself to be put down. A course in assertive, non-aggressive behavior would help you understand that you have certain rights. It may also aid you in achieving the respect and consideration you deserve by setting boundaries and not allow yourself to be put down.

Take responsibility for your feelings, and set positive goals and actions to support your new choices for behavior.

Statement 9: I love to . . .

How much time each day do you spend doing what you love? What you love contributes to your positivity and confidence. A friend of mine recently remarked that she never had time to sit down and read a good book. When we discussed her schedule, it was evident to me that she volunteered a tremendous amount of her time to her church as an accountant, Sunday school teacher, visitor to the hospital, and still more. I asked her if she was willing to give up any of her volunteer activities in order to have the time to read her book. The question gave her pause to think about what she truly valued. She loved her volunteer work, and I never heard her complain again about not getting around to the book.

Do you take time to do what you value the most? Do you love to walk? Is your favorite ritual a relaxing bubble bath with a scented candle and soft music in the background? Do you like a good round of golf and a brisk walk? Perhaps you like a Friday night to practice hockey moves?

Whatever it is that gives you pleasure and helps you relax, you are important enough to set a time each week to do it. Indulge yourself. You will be a better person for it, and those around you will appreciate the relaxed and easy-going person you become.

Statement 10: As a child, I was treated . . .

Your childhood contributes to the type of person you are growing into! Childhood should be a pleasurable learning experience of good memories. Yet we know that we can learn good things and bad things.

It is your job as an adult to sift through your own childhood experiences and learn from them. Remember the premise of a self-coaching program—learn as you go and grow into a better person. Take what was good and make it better. Take what was not good and use it as a tool for improvement.

Make Change One Day at a Time

Now you have completed the exercises and hopefully have a much better idea of the positive changes you would like to make in your life. Your goal here is to not only stretch and grow beyond feeling challenged, but to enjoy the learning. Find the positive side of each growth plan and share it with your mate. Elicit your mate's support.

- Make note of those statements that you feel are applicable to your personal experiences and feelings, and hopefully you gained insight from each.
- Review the statements again and choose one statement that you feel would make the most difference if you could change your answer into the goal you want to achieve.
- Develop one modification in sequence until you have achieved that goal. Remember to keep the goals brief and to the point. It is vital that you do not try to alter your life too much at one time. That only leaves you vulnerable to frustration and defeat.
- Once achieved, choose the next most important step and continue to work through each change.

For example, suppose you chose to work on Statement 8 in the above list: "My spouse treats me . . . " and you completed that sentence with the words, "like a child." How would you initiate your change in behavior? The first step is to recognize that you will focus on changing your behavior, not attempt to change your spouse.

Write a positive affirming statement in your journal such as *I will act as an adult and speak clearly about my feelings.* Then follow through: see yourself as an adult and act as an adult, and then determine how people view you. Are you effective in changing your manner?

Next, focus on the change you want to make and examine it from every angle. Ask yourself probing questions such as: Is this how I see myself? Do I think of myself as a child? Is my behavior indicative of an adult or of a child? Find real-life evidence to support your response.

Examine what you believe yourself to be. If you want others to perceive you as an adult, then you must see yourself as such. You must sincerely believe you are an adult and act accordingly in all situations. If you believe it—you will live it.

Look the part. Act the part. Believe in yourself. For example, if you have set a goal to act as an adult by making clear decisions, then in your mind, you are the adult who no longer allows herself to be indecisive. The day will come when you reach your goal—and it will happen because you believed in it.

Your Profile of Life Concerns

You have concerns that are your priorities because they represent problems for you. You have motivation to change what doesn't work and have more of the pleasures you enjoy! The exercises you completed earlier gave you some insight into what makes you behave the way you do. Now, it is time to prioritize a list of concerns. Use this exercise to determine what is topmost in your mind, reflecting on your social interactions with your mate, friends, and family and prioritize.

Exercise

Please rate the following list of self-concerns on a scale of 1 to 5. Number 1 indicates that the topic is of very low concern to you. Number 5 indicates that the topic is of high concern to you.

Self-concept or feelings regarding yourself	1	2	3	4	5
Relationships	1	2	3	4	5
Health	1	2	3	4	5
Money	1	2	3	4	5
Work	1	2	3	4	5
Safety	1	2	3	4	5
Appearance	1	2	3	4	5
Recreation	1	2	3	4	5

Which items in the above list concern you the most?
Which items are of utmost importance?

The answers to the two previous questions are the start for planning your priorities as mates for successfully moving through personal challenges and partnership growth issues. This entire book walks you through any personal concerns by showing you how to coach yourself through the issues. Be open to planning and prioritizing your plans for a successful partnership, and eventually for being new parents.

Your Profile of Success

If fifteen people were asked how they define success, most likely there would be fifteen different answers. Pulitzer-prize winning journalist Anna Quindlen once said, "If your success is not on your own terms, if it looks good to the world but does not feel good in your heart, it is not success at all." All too often success is equated with the amount of money a person has or some aspect of esteem or acquisition. Some people may be more concerned with quality of life. Others insist that success lies in how much you enjoy life. Believe it or not, there is a proven formula for success, and I will share it with you now:

Emotional health + social health + spiritual health = SUCCESS

It is not enough to be emotionally stable if you lack social skills and spiritual awareness. All three elements must be present for you to become a healthy, successful, and happy person. The secret is to achieve a balance between the three. To have emotional health means that you love and believe in yourself. You must be happy with the person you are. You must be willing to acquire any positive characteristics to achieve your desired results.

Exercise

Unfortunately, many people do not really know themselves. In order to give you some clues about your inner self, respond with true or false to the following statements.

1. I love to explore new places and new things. T F
2. I am happiest with familiar surroundings and friends. T F
3. I feel a need to be accepted by others. T F
4. I have a hard time controlling my temper. T F
5. I am known as an easy-going person. T F
6. I feel underappreciated in my job. T F
7. I am comfortable doing things alone. T F
8. I always seem to be in debt. T F
9. I do not enjoy exercise. T F
10. I maintain optimal health. T F
11. I believe life is "every man for himself." T F
12. I will offer a helping hand when I can. T F
13. I will help another if it serves my best interest. T F

Review the previous statements and keep in mind that everyone has different opinions of what makes them uncomfortable. For instance, the statement "I always seem to be in debt" may be bothersome to some, but may not matter to you. If you feel that your mate does not appreciate you, then you must rectify that situation in order to be a happier and more emotionally secure person. You can do this by following the eight secrets in this book for building strong relationships in preparation for new parenting.

Your Profile of Self-Worth

A belief in yourself and in what you can accomplish is crucial to how you assign and evaluate personal self-worth. Think about the following ten statements and how they relate to you. Be honest with yourself when responding. Circle either a true or false response for the following statements and record any desired notes in your journal because self-worth is necessary for effective success plans.

Exercise

	Statement		
1.	I am afraid to voice my opinions in my relationship.	T	F
2.	My mate praised me, but I didn't deserve it.	T	F
3.	I am comfortable making decisions for others.	T	F
4.	My friends look more stylish than I do.	T	F
5.	I am as well educated as my professional peers.	T	F
6.	Other people trust me with confidences.	T	F
7.	I am bothered by people who do not agree with me.	T	F
8.	I have a hard time relating to self-assured people.	T	F
9.	I know that when I set my mind to a task, I can do it.	T	F
10.	I find it difficult to accept praise.	T	F

In responding to the key elements above, you have the opportunity to see how you relate to others. Strengthening self-belief is the most important step for developing successful social skills and emotional strength. Therefore, it is crucial that you find ways to strengthen your self-belief. See Chapter 6 for the secret of self-esteem.

One powerful tool that encourages you to believe in yourself is the use of affirmations. An affirmation is a positive statement used to reframe negative feelings, observations or events. For example, if you responded "true" to negative statements in the exercise, then you should come up with a positive statement that you could repeat to yourself to counteract that negative feeling. Keep in mind that affirmations do not work by themselves and will not change you overnight, but by repeating them often, you will begin to believe in yourself and your abilities.

Challenging Statement	Positive Affirmation
My mate praised me, but I didn't deserve it.	I accept praise graciously.
I am afraid to voice my opinions.	I am willing to risk speaking up.

Return to your responses and note any that pertain to you in a negative way, and then make a list of affirmations to counteract each negative statement. This is your personal tool; it is intended to resolve the issues you have now identified. Carry the list of affirmations with you and repeat them every day and throughout the day.

When the grass always seems greener on the other side, it is not. You are seeing the world through your eyes of low self-esteem or need or discontent. The world that you see stems from your feelings about yourself and your desires for betterment. The solution is appreciation and gratitude. Remember to focus on the positive elements of your life. By looking at the positives, you can eliminate the envy and resentment that may cause your emotional pain and anxiety.

Your Plan for Change

Be willing to change. Your life becomes like a pool of stagnant water when there is no movement, change or new happenings within it. Change is the one variable that keeps life from becoming stale and boring. Change brings adventure and innovation which we review in the next chapter. Change offers the spice of life that keeps you interested and not bored.

No two people are alike, and one overall plan will not do. Your personal success plan must be tailored first to your personal needs, desires, and goals. To develop your personalized plan for change, you must take a good look at all of the information you have gathered about yourself in this chapter. Study it carefully, defining the changes you want to make in your life.

On the following chart, write down the changes you want to make in your life and list the methods you will use to bring about those changes. Also, write down some positive affirmations that you will use daily. When making your list, prioritize your highest concerns. As you practice your new lifestyle and begin to reach the goals you have set, you will be amazed at how different your life will become.

My Individual Plan for Change

Record your answers in your journal or on a separate sheet of paper.

1. Change I Would Like to Make
   Goal What do I see as the result of my change?
   Action Steps Taking one step at a time, how will I accomplish my goal?
   Positive Affirmations (to be repeated daily)

2. Change I Would Like to Make
   Goal What do I see as the result of my change?
   Action Steps Taking one step at a time, how will I accomplish my goal?
   Positive Affirmations (to be repeated daily)

Summary

In this chapter, you learned through an assessment of your individual profile where to direct your attention to change aspects of your life. By bringing your past into the picture, you received a glimpse of how it could affect your relationships with your mate and friends. You learned how to turn negatives into positives by using affirmations. You learned that success means different things to different people.

You can now give yourself the opportunity to discover what success means in your life and learn the steps you can use to reverse the negative feelings that may have impacted you. By developing your individualized plan for change, you are well on your way to becoming a happier and more successful person. You have now begun your journey toward becoming a life-coach to yourself and your success.

Wallet Card

Below, you will find some simple coaching points to remember. Read the points from the end of each chapter, then cut each card out from the back of the book and keep it with you to remind you of your goals.

- I will focus on my goals and review my action steps of my personal success plan.
- I will make one change at a time, insuring I have effective results.
- I will read and repeat my positive affirmations daily.
- Emotional + Social + Spiritual Health = SUCCESS

CHAPTER THREE

Innovation, Adventure, and Change

CHAPTER OBJECTIVES

- Cultivate a positive approach to self-coaching.
- Cultivate a positive personal attitude.
- Discard negative thought patterns and behaviors.
- Evaluate your openness to new ideas and actions.
- Discover how innovation and adventure can evoke change.
- Create a plan for adding these key elements to your life.

It is only in adventure that some people succeed in knowing themselves—
in finding themselves.

—André Gide

Succeed in Knowing Yourself

Exploration is often described as adventure. Self-exploration is no different. When self-coaching, it is the first step you will take towards defining your goals and personal success. Self-exploration will shed light on your individual strengths, weaknesses, and motivations. This will encourage you to see how your own happiness can be enhanced by embarking on a course of change in your own life. When you succeed in knowing yourself, then you will have a clearer picture of who you want to become. Change naturally follows this new knowledge and is the root of all growth—personal, professional, and relational. Although the thought of departing from your regular routine could be stressful, the outcome can produce new levels of confidence and excellence that you would never have thought possible. There is always some uncertainty associated with making a change, as no one can accurately predict the outcome.

Welcoming a new child into your family is perhaps one of the most dramatic changes that you will face. Any small step that you make in preparation for this event will help to make the transition easier. It is important to remember that change can be invigorating. If you are able to view change as offering variety, keeping life interesting and encouraging improvement, then you will be open to any opportunity for growth that life may bring. Your approach to change affects your relationship with yourself and the world around you. A positive approach is essential to understanding the importance of taking risks, making decisions, and embracing the changes that can lead to a happier, more satisfied life.

In this chapter, you will learn how to cultivate a positive approach and positive changes while discarding negative thought patterns and behaviors. You will evaluate your openness to new ideas and actions, and learn how to use your imagination to find solutions and solve problems. You will also discover how innovation and adventure can evoke change, and you will create a plan for adding these key elements to your life. All of these steps will help prepare you for the great changes that will be coming with the arrival of your child.

Embrace Change

Change is essential to personal growth. In the previous two chapters, you focused on identifying the behaviors and characteristics that make you tick. You learned that life changes are not based on willpower, but on persistent thought and action. You also learned that planning is the key to successfully coaching yourself through change. What you did not learn, however, is how your attitude towards change affects your efforts.

Change is an inevitable part of life. By accepting this, you receive the opportunity to learn, grow and discover new and different things. Change allows you to see situations and people in many lights. It also provides variety, which is essential to a rich life. When you are open to change, you are an adaptable, innovative thinker who relates well to many different types of people. In addition, you embrace change without feeling too overwhelmed or defeated in the face of unexpected events.

While it is easy to understand resisting unwelcome or unexpected change, some people shy away from all forms of change. The idea of unpredictability makes some people uncomfortable because change represents a loss of consistency, comfort, and control. It also represents a tendency to lean towards proven solutions instead of trying new and possibly more effective ones. Openness to new thoughts and ideas will give you access to limitless options to pursue your goals and enhance your life.

Use the exercise on the following page to examine your relationship with change. Keep a journal with your responses as well as any notes. For each question, pick the response that most accurately describes how you would respond to the situation. This exercise is for your own self-discovery.

Examine your Relationship with Change

1. As a college freshman, anthropology was your favorite elective.

A Because it was an easy A.

B Because you enjoy learning about other cultures.

C Because you took other classes with the professor and liked them.

2. Having your entire family over for Thanksgiving has become an enjoyable but stressful tradition.

A You continue to host because it is your duty as the oldest daughter.

B You ask your siblings to alternate years and share the responsibility.

C You continue to host because no one else can cook a turkey.

3. Your morning routine starts with brushing your teeth before breakfast. This morning, your son was sick and in the bathroom.

A You ask him to pass your toothbrush through the door.

B You ask if he needs anything before you go downstairs for breakfast.

C You stand outside the bathroom door and wait for him to finish.

4. Your boss needs a volunteer to head a new project in your area of expertise.

A You don't want the added responsibility.

B You are the first to volunteer.

C You tell her you would like to be on the team, but not lead it.

5. Your neighbor has a new puppy that burrows under the fence into your yard and digs up your rose bushes.

A You put dog training pamphlets in her mailbox.

B You talk to your neighbor and come up with several potential solutions.

C You don't say anything and hope the puppy outgrows the behavior.

6. Your company has a monthly mixer so people from other departments can get to know each other.

A You always have too much work to go.

B You always go and enjoy learning about other jobs in the company.

C You went once but there was no one there you knew, so you left.

7. As a new mother, you are often too exhausted for housework. When your husband comes home from work he often cooks dinner.

A You rarely stay awake long enough to eat it.

B You are thankful and enjoy eating the different foods he likes to cook.

C You won't eat his chicken because he doesn't cook it as long as you do.

8. You enjoy organizing the soccer carpool.

A Because it means you don't have to drive every day.
B Because it is like a great big puzzle with dozens of solutions.
C Because your way of organizing is the only one that makes sense.

9. In high school, you were in the foreign exchange program one summer.

A You have no idea what you were thinking.
B You wished you had enrolled all three years.
C You were homesick and never adjusted to the new routine.

10. You are offered a new job making significantly more money but the hours are longer.

A You are sure the human relations department has made a mistake.
B You are excited to accept and ask your family to pitch in on dinner.
C You cannot imagine yourself pulling the extra hours and meeting your household obligations.

If your responses were mostly A, you do not embrace change easily and prefer proven methods or your normal routine. If your response to most of these situations was B, you positively approach and embrace change. You accept and celebrate the many options and differences in people, places, and events. If your responses were mostly C, you resist or perhaps even fear change. This approach offers fewer opportunities for personal growth, and can lead to boredom. Try to stretch and expand your concept of change.

As with any step in your personal life-coaching plan, start slowly. Introduce a small change into your regular routine, such as trying a new restaurant or asking your spouse to help with household chores. As you accept the small changes, acknowledge your efforts and move on to bigger and bolder ones. Soon you will begin embracing change and the choices it brings.

The Importance of Innovation

Throughout time, every discovery, invention, and advancement has been the result of innovative thought. When presented with a problem or question, we all have two minds available to us—one is logical and the other is innovative or inventive. The logical mind offers up sensible, analytical solutions. The innovative mind produces a myriad of creative possibilities and options from which to choose. The logical mind favors proven methods, while the innovative one is constantly asking "What if. . . ." The logical mind uses steadfast, reasonable approaches, and the innovative mind is constantly on the lookout for new solutions to old problems.

At this point, you may be wondering what role the innovative mind plays in daily living? How does its creativity function within your home, work and social networks?

One of my clients, Mary, is a perfect example of the innovative mind at work. Mary is highly creative and a seemingly never-ending source of ideas. One of her life-coaching goals is to use her talents to promote theatre in her community. When a newly-formed improvisation group approached her to fill a volunteer public relations position, her innovative mind encouraged her to take the job. Of course, her logical mind was concerned about all the hours of work that would go uncompensated, but her innovation was looking beyond her pocketbook. It recognized that she could use this valuable experience to secure a paying position in the not too distant future.

Like Mary, you receive input from both your logical and innovative minds when presented with a problem or choice. However, if you fear change, you will ignore the untried suggestions offered to you by innovation. If you have an ingrained aversion to change, you might choose instead to lean on the familiar, even if this approach produces unsatisfactory results. Don't be discouraged if you find change uncomfortable, taking small steps may help you to incorporate minimal changes in your life rather than making a giant leap. Nothing puts a shine on lackluster results faster than learning to embrace innovation and change. When you open your mind, you can see beyond the obvious. Adventure and innovation once obscured by rigidity will present you with exciting new opportunities and multiply your chances for success.

Listen to your innovative mind and follow where it leads you. Your logical mind might try to tell you that you are being foolish, but it is not programmed for adventure. Remember that a life without adventure is a life full of yearning for a missing element.

When your mind is open to new ideas, your potential for change is tremendous. In this creative state, nothing stands between you and positive progress. The use of affirmations and relaxation techniques are two ways of nurturing innovative nature. All that you need is a guide that teaches how to change and a belief that change is possible.

Using Affirmations to Encourage Innovation

In chapter one, you learned how to use affirmations to turn negative thought patterns and behaviors into positive ones. Affirmations, which are clear statements of intent voiced for personal commitment, are great self-coaching tools. With frequent repetition, they act as positive reinforcement for thoughts and behaviors you wish to acquire or improve upon. You can create powerful changes within your mind and body when you consistently repeat affirmations with conviction and passion.

Affirmations encourage you to feel better about yourself. Changing the way you think, reprogramming your mind and removing the old negative beliefs enable you to break out of the doldrums and break into a creative new view of you!

Developing and Using Affirmations

- Base your affirmations on personal needs or goals.
- Clearly state your intent.
- State your intent in the present tense.
- Display a list of your affirmations in a place you visit frequently during the day.
- Repeat or write your affirmations throughout the day.

Exercise: Create Affirmations to Encourage Innovation

Practice creating affirmations that nurture your innovative mind. Sit quietly and slow your thinking. Use the following prompts and complete the statements with the first thought to enter your mind.

1. My innovative mind guides me . . .
2. My innovative side is . . .
3. I am open to using my innovative mind to . . .
4. My innovation helps me . . .

Using Relaxation Techniques to Encourage Innovation

When you struggle with a problem, your mind becomes a jumble. This type of turmoil makes it difficult to be innovative and see a clear solution. When you find yourself in this position, you can encourage innovation by using relaxation techniques to calm yourself, quiet your mind, and turn negative thoughts into positive ones. (See exercise on next page.)

Innovation and Risk Taking

Innovation and risk taking go hand in hand. In order to fully benefit from innovative thinking, you must be willing to take some risks. Most people avoid risks out of fear of failure or rejection. Remember that even if you do not succeed at your first attempt, the lessons you learn will make it easier to try the next time. Knowledge gained by trying something new will even affect the goals you envision for yourself.

Likewise, people who thrive on taking too many dangerous risks are also setting themselves up for failure. They will try anything, regardless of the consequences.

The key to your life-coaching balance is to use innovation tempered with logic, moderation, and balance. New paths to opportunity will open before you.

Exercise: Breathe in Relaxation and Innovation

One of the simplest paths to relaxation is deeper breathing. When we are anxious or upset, our breathing becomes rapid and shallow. This breathing pattern has a negative affect on all bodily functions including the ability to think innovatively.

To correct your breathing and ease into relaxation, you must first find a quiet spot that is free of distractions. Once in your spot, sit in a comfortable position and release as much tension as possible. Take a slow, deep breath in through your nose and notice how your stomach expands. Exhale through your mouth and contract your stomach muscles for a count of five. Use this action to push negative thoughts and energy out of your body. Repeat this exercise until you feel calmer. Once you are calm, focus your attention on your positive thoughts. Repeat affirming statements. These positive thoughts will help you understand the situation; encourage your innovative mind to produce solutions; and define your successful outcome.

During this exercise, you may envision problem areas in your life that produce negative thoughts. Here is a tool that will help loosen the hold these thoughts or memories have on your mind. Imagine a hot air balloon with a basket. Now gather up all the negative thoughts and feelings and place them in the basket. Watch as the hot air balloon slowly lifts off the ground and floats away in to the distance, carrying the negative thoughts with it. Watch until it disappears on the horizon.

Another visualization exercise that is helpful is to picture a large blackboard. Write down all of the negative thoughts in sentences on one side of the board. Now write all of the affirmations that contrast with these thoughts on the other side of the board. Erase the negative sentences so that you can only see your affirmations. With repeated use and sincere effort, these exercises will help diminish the power of negative thoughts and feelings to influence your daily life.

Slowly return to your surroundings. Take a few minutes to examine the thoughts, emotions, and reactions you experienced while in your calm state. This exercise is valuable it may help to reveal how you perceive the situation.

Note that relaxation exercises like this one may be difficult at first. Try to remain focused and not let other things pull you away. In time, as your relaxation techniques improve, innovative ideas, answers, and solutions will begin to surface and present themselves to you. As with anything that you try, the more you do it, the better you will get at it.

Francine's Story

Francine and I shared office space for several years. She was a family therapist who practiced with startling brilliance and compassion. Her approach to family dynamics was unique and made her very popular with her clients and well-respected in the professional community. A publishing house known for its self-help and psychology titles approached Francine with a book contract. They offered her a hefty advance and financial backing for an extensive promotional tour that practically guaranteed the book would be a success.

A book would take Francine's career to the next level—this truly was the chance of a lifetime. She knew that writing a book would be challenging but was confident of her ability. The book promotion, however, was another story. For all the talking Francine did for a living, she had never mastered the art of public speaking. One-on-one or in small seated groups she was fine, but she was fearful speaking to an audience.

She tried to work through her fear by attending different training courses and even undergoing hypnosis. Nothing worked, and eventually she accepted this fear as part of her makeup. Now she was at a crossroads. She could continue to accept her fear and remain in her career as it was. Or she could risk embarrassing herself in public so she could add a more challenging and stimulating facet to her career. She decided the risk was worth it.

She practiced speeches in front of the mirror and consulted public speaking coaches. She used affirmations, relaxation techniques, and creative imagery to help position herself as a confident, self-assured speaker. Still, when the time came for her first presentation, she was scared. Her mouth was dry and her hands shook as she was introduced to an audience of middle school guidance counselors. Francine walked onto the stage and just as she had imagined, she froze. She could not form a single sound. After a few seconds, someone made a joke and Francine's biggest fear came true, everyone laughed. But there was a huge difference between her fear and her reality. Instead of laughing at her, the audience was laughing with her. It had been Francine who made the joke and the laughter put her at ease enough to deliver a successful speech and complete a successful promotional tour.

Exercise: Put Things into Perspective

In order to grow and succeed, it is necessary to take risks. If you are hesitant, start by putting the situation in perspective. Personal life-coaching doesn't often include negative thinking, but in this instance it is the best starting point.

- Think of the situation you are facing in the most negative light possible.
- Now ask, what is the worst thing that could happen?
- If you take a risk and do something you have always wanted to do, will you lose face? Will you suffer rejection? Will you be a laughingstock? Does it matter if you are? Will you be considered a failure if things don't work out?

Chances are the answer to all of these questions is no. Plus, if any of these things do happen, will the world end? Again, the answer is no. What does happen when you face the worst scenario is that you are rehearsing in your mind. You are practicing responding to fear. You have faced the unknown, which is the real fear, and nothing terrible happened. In fact, you will learn from the experience, which is reason enough to take a chance.

Innovation and Decision Making

Most everything in this life requires that you be capable of making decisions. So, when developing and strengthening your innovative side, you must have solid decision-making skills.

Four Steps to Solid Decision Making

1. **Have confidence in your ability to make decisions.** No one makes the right decision every time. Instead of being afraid of being wrong, realize that you are making a decision based on what you know and what you consider to be right at the time. Then if you do make a bad choice, you will know that you did your best.
2. **Do not needlessly delay making a decision.** Have you ever dreaded doing something so badly that you put it off? The longer you put it off, the more you dreaded it. When you finally take action, you discover you are relieved to not have to think about the

issue anymore. The same goes for making decisions. If you put off making a decision, the delay may turn out to be more uncomfortable than the actual act.

3. **There are no sure things—so don't waste time looking for them.** There is no way of knowing if a decision is the right one until it is made and the results are clear. Therefore, if there is no way of knowing beforehand whether your decision is right or wrong, there is no reason to delay or worry about it. Plus, you may miss other opportunities while waiting to make a decision. Just make a sound decision based on the information you have at the time. This is your best course of action.
4. **Do not make a decision just to please others.** At one time or another we all seek approval but you should not make decisions based on the opinions of others. In order to make a solid decision, you should gather information, consider the facts and consequences, and decide on the best course of action. This ensures that you did your best and made the decision on your own.

The 99/1 Rule

Some people are indecisive. They spend so much time worrying about making the wrong decision that they make no decision at all. If this describes your behavior, then perhaps you should review the 99/1 Rule. It states that most people worry 99% of the time about things that happen only 1% of the time.

Taking Stock: Innovation and Adventure

Innovation represents creative thought and action. Adventure is your willingness to try new things and experiment with your innovative thoughts and put them into action. Individuals with open minds actively pursue and engage innovation. They are also more receptive to new methods and initiate necessary life changes. In short, they are more adventurous.

Assess Your Adventurous Nature

How willing are you to try new things? To fully understand the role innovation plays in your life, your answer will reveal your enthusiasm. Does your innovative mind offer you creative solutions on one hand while your logical mind bats it down with the other? Or are you the type of person who will try anything once?

Use the following assessment tool to analyze your personal adventure profile. The results can be used in your self-coaching program as an indicator of the change necessary for personal improvement, as well as for the stage of life you are about to embark on.

Exercise

Answer each of these true or false questions in your journal along with any thoughts that come up as you read them.

1. I like to try new hobbies and learn different activities. T F
2. I am comfortable starting conversations with new people. T F
3. My dream is to own and drive a racecar. T F
4. All of my pants are black and easy to coordinate with outfits. T F
5. My idea of a great vacation would be shark diving in Belize. T F
6. I tend to frequent restaurants where I know I will like the food. T F
7. At social functions, I stay close to friends. T F
8. I volunteer for challenging assignments at work. T F
9. I am willing to visit a strange city without hotel reservations. T F
10. My favorite amusement park ride is the roller coaster. T F
11. I would rather watch sports than participate. T F
12. I don't answer the telephone during thunderstorms. T F
13. I think mountain climbers are crazy. T F
14. I dislike traveling alone. T F
15. I would like to learn to pilot my own plane. T F

Results

Adventurous: Your response to statements 1, 2, 3, 5, 8, 9, 10, and 15 was True. You are very adventurous and willing to try new things. You are most excited when you have no idea what lies beyond the next bend.

Reasonable: Your response to statements 4, 6, 7, 11, 12, 13, and 14 was True. You are solid and reliable, but not quick to try new things. Your motto is better to be safe than sorry.

Balanced: If your responses were mixed, you have a healthy balance of adventure and sensibility. You are willing to try some new things to keep life interesting and your relationships fresh.

Adding Innovation and Adventure to Your Life

Now that you have learned the importance of innovation and adventure, it is time to add these key elements to your personal life-coaching plan. In your journal, begin by listing some innovative ideas you would like to experiment with or adventures you would like to try. Next to each idea or activity write a detailed description of the steps you will take to achieve this goal. For instance, if you have always wanted to learn how to play the guitar, your first step may be to visit a music store and try different guitars for the right fit. Then you may want to enroll in lessons or buy an instructional video to learn from.

Exercise

Open your mind and add innovation and adventure to your life. Use these guidelines to list your innovative goals and the steps you plan to take towards achieving them in your journal. Be sure to break your process down into manageable parts and celebrate every small step you take.

My Individual Plan for Innovation and Adventure

Write your answers in your journal or on a separate sheet of paper.

Innovative Idea/Adventure I Want to Try:
Example: Learn about Spanish culture.

Ways I Can Achieve This:
Example: Visit a Latino grocery store—enroll in a Spanish class

Organizing Your Desired Personal Life Changes

In the first two chapters, you spent time getting to know yourself and identifying changes you wanted to make in your life. This chapter has offered you additional information on the importance of innovation, adventure, risk taking, and decision-making. Now it is time for you to review what you have learned so far, organize your intentions, and apply this to your Individual Plan for Change.

Begin by reviewing the changes you outlined at the end of chapter two. Look at your affirmations and what steps you plan to take towards making these changes. In light of your new knowledge, can you think of other innovative ways to achieve your goals? Would strengthening your decision-making skills or improving your innovative thought processes be of help? Are there areas where you need to take more risks?

Next, prioritize your list of changes. Place the changes you feel are most important at the top of the list and concentrate on them first. Remember that change is a slow and deliberate process, so only undertake one change at a time.

When you decide which change is the most important, ask yourself why you want to make that particular change? Why do you behave in that manner and what can you do to change it? What positive behaviors that relate to this change are you keeping?

Finally, identify the steps you need to take in order to accomplish each change. Then make that change happen. Once you have grown accustomed to the new behavior, practice it until it becomes part of your personality. Eventually, you will realize that changing is not as difficult as you once perceived it to be. Remember that the new baby will bring enormous changes; therefore any steps you want to make in innovation should be very small.

Summary

In this chapter, you explored the effect that adventure and innovation have on personal change. You assessed your sense of adventure and learned how to self-coach yourself through the changes necessary to become more innovative. You also acquired two tools, affirmations and relaxation techniques, to help you nurture your innovative mind.

You also learned how important embracing change, risk taking and decision making are to improving your life or fine tuning the areas of your life that you want to enhance. Finally, you reviewed, organized, and improved upon your Individual Plan for Change.

Wallet Card

- Don't be afraid to make change one step at a time.
- Trust my innovative mind.
- Repeat my positive affirmations, and modify them as life changes.
- Prioritize changes to be made.
- Look for ways to add adventure and innovation to my life, and then write down my goals to create innovation.

CHAPTER FOUR

Using Your Life Experiences to Set Success Goals

CHAPTER OBJECTIVES

- Learn to incorporate the traits of successful people into your personal success plan.
- Learn what true management skills are and how they fit into your life.
- Assess your success skills.
- Develop goals to strengthen your success skills.
- Learn to manage your resources like time, money, and energy effectively for your success.

Without goals and plans to reach them, you are like a ship that has set sail with no destination.

—F. Dodson

The secret of success is constancy to purpose.

—Benjamin Disraeli

There Are Secrets to Success

In this chapter, you will continue your journey toward self-improvement by learning how to use management skills successfully in your life. You may associate the word "management" with business, and the word has much broader application for your personal life and relationships as you will see in this chapter. The term management means to handle something effectively, to use resources well, or the act of controlling something with skill. If you could be savvy in handling tough decisions and controlling your life by effectively managing your resources like time, money, and energy, then you will have the foundations for success.

I will show you how to assess your success skills in order to identify areas where you can be innovative and bring about positive changes. You will design a success plan to lead you to desired goals, inner harmony, and an organized, purposeful life. The guidelines that follow will set you on the right path and help ease your way through any resistance that you face when you meet life's tougher management challenges.

All Challenges Are Learning Experiences

No one likes to deal with tough situations or unpleasant people. However, every problem, no matter how large or small, can and should be used as a learning experience. Once you meet the problem head on and find a solution, then you will know how to handle similar issues in the future. At this point in your life it is vital that you are able to change. There will be many times when a tried and true method of coping will not work once the baby arrives.

In fact, each time you face adversity and succeed in solving the issue, you have developed a new strategy for success. Each new strategy makes you a more resilient, resourceful problem-solver. You may not realize how much ability you already have in solving a problem or dealing with another's negative attitude. You have the knowledge; often finding solutions is really remembering what skills have worked for you previously to get the results you desired.

Remember that no problem is insurmountable. How you tackle the problem determines your outcomes. You can either escalate the problem into a major issue or find solutions that satisfy all parties involved. How you deal with a problem helps determine the solution. Remember the inner wisdom you have already developed and bring it forth.

Stay in Alignment with Your Success Plan

In preparing yourself through personal life-coaching, by setting goals and developing your life-plan changes, you will know the proper way to address issues and problems that might arise in your partnership or as a new parent. Life-coaching will not eliminate your problems, but it will arm you with the proper tools to meet obstacles head on. It will also build your confidence and self-esteem. Here is a story of one woman who used her success plan to make an important decision.

Miriam's friend, Rachel, invited her to travel to a luxury Belize resort for a "Girls-Only Vacation" with her and two other female acquaintances. Miriam was ready to leap at the opportunity, so hungry was she for a break from work and the tedium of graduate school. The holidays were a perfect time to take off from the world. Yet, as a single woman, Miriam was expected and had always visited her parents' home for the holiday celebrations.

Miriam was confused, but also had the confidence to face the choices and set aside her fear. Using her coaching skills, she listed the pros and cons of each choice. Was she willing to risk the disapproval of her family, her father's anger, and "hearing about it" until the next holiday season? Maybe, the thought of such a conversation fluttered in her stomach. Did she have the confidence to speak to her family clearly about her need as an adult woman for rest, relaxation, and freedom from the school and work pressures for two weeks? Yes, she had often talked over tough decisions that she faced with her family, and they were supportive. The difference now was that her family may not consider her going on this vacation as "responsible" behavior. After all, it wasn't like going to graduate school.

Miriam recalled her personal value of independence and reviewed the goals of her personal coaching plan. In alignment with her success plan, Miriam chose to take the vacation with friends and forgo the family holiday celebrations.

The Art of Compromise When Necessary

What if your success plan goals clash with other people's expectations for you? Like Miriam, perhaps you feel pulled between two sets of values or expectations that others have for your behavior. If you ever feel pulled on by others or people make you feel obligated to meet their expectations, there are three important points to remember:

1. Follow the values and goals that you list in your success plan.
2. Like Miriam, look at your options with confidence and weigh the pros and cons of each decision. Do not back away from conversation about your decisions.
3. Remember the art of compromise.

Compromise is settling differences, usually by each side offering a concession or an alternative to their expectations. For example, after Miriam decided to follow her personal plan and take the vacation, she shared her decision with her family. She was surprised at their genuine support for her need to relax.

Her Mom asked if she could take a three-day weekend in February and visit with them at the family's beach house, which was always a serene place in winter. What a great idea! Miriam so appreciated her family's support without pressure that she took delight in planning the family weekend.

The art of compromise has several levels. The first is that you must make your decisions from confidence, strength, and within your game plan for success. The second level is that when you come from strength and self-respect, others will respect you in turn. Like Miriam, you may be surprised when those who have other expectations for you really support your decision without hassle. The third level is that compromise has to be a win-win for both parties. If Miriam had agreed to a three-day weekend with her parents out of pressure, she would have resisted going and found excuses to stay home.

The art of compromise is a life-coaching strategy that empowers you to honor and stick to your success plan. It enables others to negotiate a win-win situation with you.

Ten Traits of Successful People

Studies show that successful people exhibit ten common traits that can bolster you to achieve your dreams. Examine these ten traits and determine which are your strengths and which qualities challenge you to grow. Bring the best of yourself to your relationship as well as new parenting. Below, you will find each success trait followed by a life-coaching tip you can use to strengthen your skills. The qualities of character demonstrated by successful people are:

1. Positive thinking
2. Documenting goals
3. Taking action
4. Continuous learning
5. Practicing persistence
6. Attention to details
7. Remaining focused on time and money
8. Daring to be different
9. Perfecting the art of communication
10. Taking responsibility for your actions

Success Trait 1: Positive thinking

The reason that positive thinking has such incredible power is because you cannot fake it. People may not realize how transparent they can appear to others by wearing their emotions on their sleeve. We can see people's feelings in their eyes, and their thoughts can appear through their facial expressions. One's innermost thoughts will always come through and affect behavior.

If you get into the habit of thinking positively, you will receive positive results. You will appear positive and vibrant to others. Researchers in positive psychology indicate that persons who are committed to positive thinking notice an immediate improvement in their energy and attitude.

A team that takes the field with negative thoughts such as, "This other team is so much better than we are. We don't have a chance," probably will not win. A good coach teaches his team to think positively. The coach will give the team members a winning attitude, so they are ready to take on the challenge of the game. You, too, can be ready for challenges with a positive attitude. Even if you do not win, you will know to use the learning experience for your personal growth.

Use your life-coaching skills to stay focused in a positive direction. **Remember, a positive attitude wins every time by the sheer power of your thinking.**

> **Life Coaching Tip:** Stop immediately when you start thinking negatively about a particular situation. Search diligently for a positive aspect of the situation and grab onto it, no matter how insignificant it appears. Focus and concentrate on the positive aspect until the negative thinking is gone. You will see how to resolve and learn from the problem.

Success Trait 2: Documenting goals

If you want to be effective in your success plan, then you must write your goals in a specific, precise manner. Next, document your goals.

How will you know if you reach your goal? How will you *feel* when you reach the goal and what *behavior* will you demonstrate when the goal is achieved? By documenting concrete feelings and actions, you are more likely to focus and achieve them. Use specific language when documenting your goals. It does no good to say, "I want a good job with a high salary this year." Instead, you should write, "I will have a professional job as an architect and will earn $150,000 this year."

At the end of Chapter One, you created an individual plan for change in which you documented some behaviors that you would like to change for your personal growth and the action steps to accomplish them. You completed the same steps at the end of Chapter Two. At the end of Chapter Three, you developed and documented ways to be innovative and to cultivate a sense of adventure. All of these action plans are examples of having definitive goals and documenting the steps for achieving those goals.

Life Coaching Tip: Review the plans that you developed at the end of previous chapters. Are your goals clear and definitive? Are the action plans still viable? Make any changes now to update this material.

When confronted with a new idea, sit down with your journal. At the top of the paper, write down the idea and mark it as a goal. List all of the pros and cons of that goal. If you decide that the pros outweigh the cons, then list the steps necessary to see the idea through to completion.

Success Trait 3: Taking action

You have learned that you must act on your goals in order to see results. Sometimes you may not feel like taking action or you find yourself resistant to your progress. What can you do to motivate yourself? First you could leverage your fears. Sometimes if you envision the result of taking no action, you get motivated quickly to move on with your success plan.

Here is a real life example from Tracy's pregnancy success plan:

Goal: To communicate and decide with my mate about which classes to take for pregnancy preparation.

My resistance to my goal: He'll make excuses about having the time. Maybe he isn't really interested in going through this pregnancy with me. That he doesn't care enough to study with me and make preparations. That he'll think the whole pregnancy is my job.

Fears: If I don't have this conversation and take action on this goal, all my worst fears will come true: I'll never know if he cares enough to participate and really wants this pregnancy. I'll be all by myself and won't have any loving support. I'll get depressed and have a sad, depressed baby.

You can see that the more fears Tracy listed, the worst the scenario grew in her mind of not taking action on her goal. She mentally looked at the worst scenario and played it through in her mind. Looking at fears in this way is called leveraging, and it is a positive force to motivate you to action. Look at your goals and study your plans. Decide today to take whatever action is necessary to begin your journey toward successful new parenting.

Life Coaching Tip: Never procrastinate. Begin immediately to act on the steps outlined in your plan. The sooner you act, the more likely you are to achieve your goals.

Success Trait 4: Continuous learning

The one specific trait of successful people is that they love to learn. They equate learning with growth, expansion and freedom. One Chinese proverb states that learning is like rowing upstream; not to advance is to drop back.

There is no such thing as having too much knowledge and the key to issues like solving problems or managing stress is to find accurate information and apply it. Keep learning in every way possible. Learn to rely on your own knowledge so you do not have to be dependent upon others when making important decisions.

> **Life Coaching Tip:** Make it a priority to take at least one course each year. It may be something you always wanted to explore for fun, such as oil painting; or it may be a training course to help with your career, such as website design. No matter what you to choose to learn, it will be advantageous to you throughout your life.

Success Trait 5: Practicing persistence

What is worthwhile in your life may not come easily, and how you successfully maneuver through the rough spots makes the difference between failure and success. Persistence is the trait that you bring to self-coaching to make your goals successful. Persistence means to be diligent, keep your focus and don't give up. A marketing guru who went from being a high school coach to a multimillionaire in eleven years responded this way when I asked what his secret for financial success was, "Whatever you are working on, focus on it each and every day. If you are marketing, then put in one hour every day on that task. If you are writing a book, then each day, make an effort to contribute to that goal. When my son wanted to learn tennis, we went to the tennis court every day for one hour so he understood from a very young age what was required for success. Today he could be a world champion should he pursue that path." This savvy businessperson was persistent. First, like the multimillionaire, you have to decide that you will be diligent, and then schedule the time and put in the effort.

Focus your time effectively for what you want and never stop trying. Believe every minute that you can achieve your dreams. What you accomplish depends on you. If you persist, the results will be that much sweeter when they arrive. The following is a real life example of persistence from a new mother.

Jessica's Story

Jessica had never been too happy with her weight before her pregnancy, but her postpartum body was sending her into the depths of self-criticism and despair. She felt it was almost impossible to keep on top of her eating habits with her new daughter, Chloe, dictating her schedule. Even if she could find the time, exercising did not seem like an option initially because she'd had a C-section.

Jessica was feeling bad about herself, but she could usually avoid the tears that would well up in her eyes when she examined her reflection, knowing that the time she wasn't spending on herself was spent giving love and attention to Chloe. However, as Jessica and her husband developed a household routine, Jessica made some tentative efforts to lose the pregnancy weight. Unfortunately, her metabolism had slowed dramatically, and there were no quick results to reinforce her efforts. Jessica felt so unattractive that her puzzled husband could not understand why a few casual compliments and words of encouragement were met with anger and tears.

Finally, Jessica sought help from her doctor. With the help of a nutritionist, she developed a weight loss program that she could stick to. She found a way to eat her meals at the proper times; and she discovered that she could get some great exercise by taking walks with Chloe. Everyone in the family benefited from the well-balanced time schedule. Jessica's spirits were uplifted and she persisted in her efforts until her body looked better than ever.

Life Coaching Tip: When you encounter a problem that seems to be overwhelming, do not give up. Roll up your sleeves, work hard and stick with it. You will be amazed at the results you can achieve.

Success Trait 6: Attention to details

What if you are persistent, and yet, you are unable to reach some of your goals? Sometimes failure happens if you forget to pay attention to the details. The overlooking of details can become the stumbling block to success as was Jason's problem. Jason is an entrepreneur in that he works as an independent salesperson for a home remodeling corporation. Jason is the most successful salesperson for the entire company because he loves people and he is a great networker. People respond to Jason's charm like magic. In addition to his charm, Jason knows his business. He can answer any question about remodeling and constructing homes, even those that most homeowners seeking advice don't know to ask. Jason completes several sales a day, and then becomes bogged down in stacks of paperwork. Filling out the items sold, remembering to fill in the customer's demographic data and other such information details drives Jason to distraction, quite literally. Because Jason knows his strengths and challenges through his personal self-coaching program, he spends his time with people where he is most effective. To solve the challenge of his focus to detail, he hired an assistant to fulfill the paperwork.

Strive to become a detail-orientated person. Be familiar with every aspect of a project so that you can take control of the situation and head off any problems before they pop up. The overlooking of details can become the stumbling block to success as the following example demonstrates.

Scott and Marilyn

Scott and Marilyn were very enthusiastic about their pregnancy. They were both conscientious about researching prenatal care, hospitals, drug interactions and every other thing that could cause anxiety in an expectant couple. They carefully considered the duration of Marilyn's maternity leave from her job and planned their budget accordingly. With all of their care and attention to the arrival of the baby, they forgot to look into the complicated paperwork necessary to apply for the temporary disability insurance that Marilyn was entitled to during her leave. When their son was born, they had much less time to get the information needed from her employer and submit the application. They both experienced needless panic and a delay in receiving benefits as a result of letting details go unattended to.

The moral of this story is that it is good to pay attention to details, but you must also look at the big picture. Write things down and make checklists. This will keep you on track and will also make you feel accomplished when you can check items off on the list. Strive to become a detail-orientated person. Practice looking at all the aspects of a project so that you can take control of the situation and head off any problems before they pop up.

> **Life Coaching Tip:** Examine all angles of any project. It will not take long for this skill to become a life habit.

Success Trait 7: Remaining focused on your time and your money

Time and money are two things that could deplete you if you do not focus specifically on these aspects of your life. As a successful person, others may ask you to donate your time or money to their organizations or causes. Choose one and use your time for that special cause. The same is true of money so be selective in your donation. Which specific work or organization calls to you?

Incorporate quality time for yourself into your weekly routine. Whether it is time by yourself that brings soothing to a busy day or time spent with your mate in quiet conversation, don't let this goal slip through your fingers.

> **Life Coaching Tip:** Become a person who leads a well-rounded life. Allow time for work, play, and personal fulfillment.

Success Trait 8: Daring to be different

Confidence and courage are the necessary ingredients to attempt a new, innovative idea or project. A good leader will accept challenges and reach for the horizon. Respected business author Theodore Levitt said, "Just as energy is the basis of life itself, and ideas the source of innovation, so is innovation the vital spark of all human change, improvement and progress." To be innovative is to be different. To speak up and express new ideas at the risk of being daring is a sign of success. Taking the idea and moving it into action makes progress happen. You be the one to accept the challenge of daring to be different.

Life Coaching Tip: Accept challenges and do your best to meet them. Never back away from a new idea or venture unless you are convinced it will be harmful or illegal. Keep a journal of your new experiences, so you can look back and be inspired as you remember how you felt during those experiences.

Success Trait 9: Perfecting the art of communication

Communication is a two-way process of speaking and listening. Consider the fact that each person who initiates a communication is responsible for the completion of the process. Often the person communicating will finish the message and assume that the person who received the message and understood the content. Such a scenario is not always true, and very common in relationships and in families. Always check in with the other person in your conversation, dialogue or meeting. Asking a question like, "Did I communicate clearly?" or "Did you get that?" is helpful for clarity. With children, you can ask them to repeat what you told them in their own way, or ask a question which clarifies their understanding, "So are we agreed that you will go straight home from school? What time shall I expect you?" When you listen to others, they will feel valued. When you insure that they got your message, they will value you.

Life Coaching Tip: Pay close attention to people you consider to be good communicators. Make note of what they do. Study how they speak and how they listen. Learn how to improve your own communication skills by observing good communicators.

Success Trait 10: Taking responsibility for your actions

Being responsible for your actions is the most important success trait that you can possess. Being responsible is the cornerstone upon which the other nine traits rest. If you are responsible then you have integrity and honor your word. People can depend upon you because you stick to your commitment. Give credit where credit is due and do not blame others if things do not go as expected. Tony Robbins said, "Put yourself in a state of mind where you say to yourself, 'Here is an opportunity for me to celebrate like never before, my own power, and my own ability to get myself to do whatever is necessary.'" Being responsible ultimately implies that you can depend on yourself and trust yourself to carry through.

> **Life Coaching Tip:** Responsibility and success go hand-in-hand. Together, they can make you a powerful figure who leads a life others will want to emulate.

An Assessment of Your Success Skills

Are you ready for success? Most people want it, desire it, and plan for it, yet have old habits that stand in their way. To find out which success skills you already possess, and which skills you need to develop, fill out the following questionnaire.

Exercise

Below are eleven true or false statements. After you respond to the statements, then assess your answers. From this assessment, you will be initiating specific changes for personal improvement in your success plan. Decide if the following statements are true or false for you.

1. I enjoy new experiences.	T	F
2. I am receptive to new ideas and ways.	T	F
3. I am achievement-oriented.	T	F
4. I am action-oriented.	T	F
5. I am a goal setter.	T	F
6. I focus on maximizing my potential.	T	F
7. I am committed to lifetime learning.	T	F
8. I am detail-oriented.	T	F
9. I am considered to be good.	T	F
10. I believe in the value of teamwork.	T	F
11. I rate my self-esteem in the normal range.	T	F

Next, as you review your assessment, make note of the statements to which you responded with "false." To develop your success potential to the fullest, then work on these areas. Make the statement into a specific goal, and add action steps to your planning. For example:

Statement: I am considered to be good.

Goal: I will try one new behavior each week in which I can succeed. I will see myself as good and affirm this through positive thinking.

Action Steps: (1) Go to the putting green and practice putting. (2) Persist in this behavior once a week until I am good or happy with my success. (3) Go to the driving range and practice my drives. (4) Persist in this behavior until I feel good about my skill level. (5) Get a golf game together with the guys and play 9 holes. Look for skills improvement, a better score, or feedback from my foursome.

- A successful you will enjoy new experiences and will be receptive to new ideas. That is innovation!
- Move ahead with your success plan, consistently looking to achieve.
- Commit yourself to learning to maximize your potential.
- Be detail-oriented, as a good communicator always works well with others.
- Think highly of yourself before you can expect another's respect.

Each time you accomplish a project successfully, it will compel you to try even more new ideas. Review these success principles, keeping in mind which ones you will incorporate into your success plan at the end of this chapter.

Success Statement 1: I am open and excited to try new experiences.

Successful people always experience the ups and downs of accomplishments and failures, becoming the sum of many experiences. This is the journey of personal growth and gaining the knowledge that is necessary for personal success. As you learn from trial and error, each new experience teaches you a lesson that is a useful step on the climb up the Pyramid of Success.

Success does not come from confinement or stagnation, but from a willingness to listen to new and different ideas and experiment with them. Remember, no experience is a wasted one.

Success Statement 2: I am intrigued by new ideas and willing to experiment.

As your own life coach, I encourage you to participate in activities that provide for your success plan. Need ideas in marketing, fashion, or relationships? Maybe you are afraid of failure in stretching beyond your comfort zone. Be an example to others around you, life lessons can be learned from successes as well as failures—everything is a learning experience.

Success Statement 3: I set goals and focus consistently to achieve them.

Without goals, you would drift through life in an aimless fashion. Goals allow you to know where you want to go and develop a roadmap for the journey. The foundation of finding the necessary means to achieve goals should be established early in your success plan. In Chapter One you reviewed what motivated you. Call upon your motivation to make consistent efforts with your goals. Don't shrug them off. Proper planning helps you achieve goals.

Success Statement 4: The idea of learning excites me.

Knowledge is power. When you prepare for your success plan by educating yourself, anticipating problems, and finding solutions, you arm yourself for life's challenges. Good learning habits will provide you not only with information, but also with the self-confidence necessary to be successful.

Success Statement 5: I communicate effectively.

Skilled communicators have the ability to share their ideas in such a way as to ensure that others understand them. Developing the skills to critically construct your thoughts and communicate them effectively is the cornerstone of this trait.

Success Statement 6: I work well individually and as part of a team.

Some of us prefer to work alone. A prudent and successful work skill is to be a member of a team also. The more successful person can do both well and communicate boundaries as necessary. People will work better and more willingly with a team player than with a loner. It takes a team to build success. While it is a valuable tool to be able to work alone and be autonomous, it is equally important to understand that there are times when it takes more than one person to do a job. Even better, valuing and appreciating your team members is a strong success trait.

Success Statement 7: I generally feel good about myself.

I have mentioned previously in this book that self-confidence is the foundation of success. If you doubt your abilities or any other facet of your life, you can gain the confidence you need to succeed through experience. Step out, take a risk, learn something new and put it to use. For example, if you do not feel confident in giving presentations, then practice speaking aloud in front of a mirror. Find ways to experience speaking next in smaller groups and develop the encouragement to move to the next level.

Success Statement 8: I am comfortable in the role of leader.

If you grew up with support and have knowledge and self-confidence, you probably assumed leadership roles naturally. Do you need to learn specific leadership skills? Then consider seminar or training classes to develop those areas of your interest.

Improving Your Success

In Chapter One, you learned the equation for individual success:

Emotional health + Social health + Spiritual health = SUCCESS

You thought about what it means for you and thought about your own model for success. Remember, no two people want or need the same things to make them feel successful.

In this chapter, you assessed your success skills. Now, you are going to organize and document your plan for success. To design a plan to suit you, you must think again about what it is you desire. This is important, because you cannot move forward effectively until you have figured out what you want and need.

Sit in a quiet place with no distractions. In your journal, document your plan for success by writing a list of successes you would like to achieve. List what you need to do, as a leader, in order to achieve each success definition. Feel free to write down multiple ways of achieving that success.

When making your list, prioritize the items. Take it one step at a time. Never attempt to tackle more than one change at a time. Good luck and have fun marking your road to success!

A Success Plan for Me

Write your answers in your journal or on a separate sheet of paper.

Success I Would Like to Achieve:
Example: Develop my ability to take care of myself with daily exercise after the baby is born

Ways I Can Achieve This Success:

1. Hire a babysitter three times a week for a few hours in order to participate in daily exercise.
2. Take personal training.

Summary

In this chapter, you learned about the common traits of successful people and how to incorporate these secrets into your life.

You conducted an assessment to measure your readiness for success. By looking at the results, you identified areas you need to work on in order to achieve success. In this chapter, you documented a success plan for yourself.

Wallet Card

- I value challenges and failures as learning experiences.
- I set goals, follow them, review them, and update them.
- I communicate effectively.
- I keep a positive attitude.
- I am persistent in my endeavors.

PART TWO

THE FIRST ACTION GOALS FOR NEW PARENTS

Putting your goals into action with your mate and integrating those goals into your lives

CHAPTER FIVE

New Parents and Styles

Introduction to the 8 Secrets to Success for Yourself, Your Mate, and Your New Family

---

CHAPTER OBJECTIVES

- Understand the transition from being mates in a relationship to being partners in parenthood.
- Be aware of the three stages of pregnancy and the effect on you as a couple.
- Understand current parenting styles.
- Determine your personal parenting style.
- Understand the 8 secrets to becoming successful new parents.
- Evaluate your self-perceived skills in each area of the 8 secrets.

Parents who expect change in themselves as well as in their children, who accept it and find in it the joy as well as the pains of growth, are likely to be the happiest and most confident parents.

—Fred Rogers

You have explored a diversified path to self-improvement in the first four chapters. You have learned how to:

- Identify strengths and weaknesses.
- Target changes that facilitate desired goals.
- Create and implement your individual success plans.

These fundamental life-coaching practices make it possible for you to align your actions, goals, and desires now. They help you organize your intentions so that you may live harmoniously and with purpose.

These practices remain constant and invaluable even as life evolves and goals change. Every life is a series of changes. Individual choice plays an instrumental role in making these life transitions smooth and fun. Self-coaching tools are designed to illuminate your choices and outline your options for success. They are a roadmap to help you see where you have been, where you are going, and how you will get there.

In this chapter you will enhance your self-coaching skills around parenting styles and values. Then you will understand what your parenting style could be and determine your level of understanding of and comfort with the eight secrets to being successful new parents.

The Transition to Parenthood

One of the most significant life transitions occurs when mates become parents. From the moment of conception, a child stretches the boundaries of intimacy. Immediately, the one-on-one relationship begins to evolve and expand until the couple becomes a family. This transition is not immediate or magical. What is magical, however, is that the transition to pregnancy and parenthood seem to be two halves of a whole.

As the embryo grows, develops, and changes, so do her parents. The prospect of bringing a new life into the world is at once awe-inspiring and daunting. It also brings with it a sense of urgency that requires couples to retreat and reorganize. Many expectant parents begin their pregnancy with a sense of ambivalence. Even if the child has been eagerly anticipated and well planned, couples often experience conflicting emotions. This uncertainty produces feelings of guilt and causes new mothers and fathers to worry for the sake of their unborn child. Many parents-to-be expect conception to provide them with strength and all-consuming love. They believe they will naturally and spontaneously become their ideal of the perfect parent. In reality, while conception makes a couple parents, parenthood is an evolving relationship that lasts a lifetime. Parenthood is the ultimate growth experience, and your self-coaching skills will offer strategies to explore this new experience and step forward gracefully to live it.

Pregnancy in Stages

Parents-to-be undergo a great many changes during the course of a pregnancy. It takes a full nine months for couples to physically and psychologically prepare for the arrival of their child. Parents of children born prematurely report feeling as if they were not ready to become mothers and fathers, that their transition was somehow incomplete. Even though there is no magical formula, the expectation that there will be nine months to prepare for parenthood is ingrained as part of the cultural experience. Therefore, when that time is cut short, couples can feel ill prepared and apprehensive about their ability to rise to the occasion that the birth of their child begins.

Pregnancy itself can be divided into three distinct stages—Acceptance, Separation and Exploration. These psychological stages coincide with the obvious physical changes in both mother and child. Identifying them helps expectant parents physically and mentally make room in their life for a baby.

Acceptance

In the first stage of pregnancy, couples learn to accept the reality and responsibility of parenthood. Initially, many people feel ambivalent about the matter. Even if the couple is dedicated to becoming a family, the first few months of their pregnancy can be emotionally tumultuous. This may be especially true for the mother who is also dealing with physical symptoms such as morning sickness and exhaustion.

Stages of Acceptance for Mothers-to-be

Overcome ambivalence In the beginning, both parents may experience feelings of ambivalence, but for the mother overcoming this feeling and any anxiety that comes with it is essential. She will begin to perceive the baby as perfect and very much wanted. This positive thinking helps her to overcome any negativity and guilt stemming from her earlier ambivalence.

Enlist help in understanding powerful emotions Women yearn to understand the powerful emotions that accompany pregnancy. They want to know how these emotions may be preparing them for parenthood. This makes them start searching for support in the form of doctors, nurses and experienced mothers.

Withdraw to reorganize The physical and emotional process of pregnancy requires a great deal of energy. Therefore, women often withdraw in order to reorganize and bring balance to their lives. It may be that she feels forced into motherhood, even if she very much wants children. She may blame her mate for impregnating her and for the responsibility they must now assume. Thoughts such as these are all part of her initial ambivalence, and it may be necessary for her to withdraw in order to process them. Luckily, these feelings will pass.

Accept the embryo as part of her body At first, both the body and mind view the embryo as a foreign object. The mother may have negative feelings about her mate, seeing the embryo as an intrusion on his part. Eventually, however, her hormones change, the body accepts and begins to nurture the growing baby as does her mind and spirit. Some women may not experience this stage at all.

Accept the role of motherhood The end result of this initial stage of pregnancy is the acceptance of motherhood and the responsibility of bringing a child into the world.

Separation

During the fifth month of gestation, parenthood is solidified. It is at this point that the mother actually feels her child for the first time. The movements produce what is termed stroking sensations, also called quickening. Reaching this stage is monumental to the pregnancy. This movement is the first indication that the embryo is a separate being. It may also be the earliest time of bonding between mother and child. Once the separation is established, a clear delineation between mother and child exists. Now there can be a relationship and the quickening is the child's first contribution.

Separation also helps expectant mothers acknowledge the role their mates have in the process. In the early stages of pregnancy, it is easy for a mother to consider the baby hers alone. While that may be a powerful feeling, it can also be overwhelming. Separating herself from the embryo and recognizing the role of father can alleviate her fears of inadequacy. It reassures her and emphasizes her role as a parenting mate.

Exploration

During the last months of pregnancy, parents-to-be continue to see the fetus as an individual. As quickening turns into kicks and flips, both mother and father become wholly aware of the child as a member of the family. This is when names are picked, nurseries are painted, and childcare is discussed. There is no longer any doubt that the couple will soon be parents.

The acceptance of this fact leads to the personification of the fetus. At this point, the baby is playing an active role in the forming of relationships. As her activity levels increase and fall into regular patterns, the mother begins to recognize and anticipate them. Because this activity is forceful and evident, the father is also able to participate in the physical sensations associated with parenthood at this stage. The expectant parents may assign their child a temperament and personality in relation to these patterns. Fetal activity becomes a way of interacting with the soon-to-be born baby. For instance, the child may kick like a soccer player, move like a dancer, bang around like a drummer, or sit like a lump on mom's bladder. By identifying and labeling patterns such as these, parents are interacting with and personifying their baby so she will not be a stranger at birth. Let's look at this real-life problem and see how this couple resolved their issues.

Anatomy of a New Parent's Dilemma

Alicia and Bob had been married for three years when they conceived. Even though they had always planned to have children, they were surprised when it actually happened. Since Alicia exhibited no morning sickness, exhaustion or change in routine, both she and Bob remained ambivalent towards the pregnancy. In fact, there were even moments when Bob would forget that he was soon going to be a father. At the stage of being four months pregnant, Alicia was still wearing her size 8 jeans and pulling late nights working at her media management job.

But things were starting to change. The changes were not so much external as they were internal. She was feeling differently and tried to talk to Bob about it, but he could not relate. In addition, since she was showing no outward signs of pregnancy, Bob was not feeling the tug of parenthood. While it was true that Alicia was just beginning to accept their future role as parents, she resented what she perceived as Bob's irresponsibility. Likewise, he resented her newly adopted judgmental nature and tendency to brood. This resentment increased and manifested into withdrawal on the part of both Alicia and Bob.

Both mates might expect in a pregnancy that they will accept the responsibility of parenthood. It doesn't usually occur at the exact same time, however. It is also expected that because the mother is dealing with the physical aspects of the process that she will feel a greater need to reconcile any feelings of ambivalence. Both of these situations were in play with Alicia and Bob. Strong communication skills were absent.

On the one hand, it is not necessary for this couple to completely grasp all of the psychological changes they will experience before they experience them. On the other hand, it is vitally important that they learn how to communicate effectively. Strong communication skills will promote empathy within the relationship and encourage both of them to participate fully in the pregnancy. See Chapter Seven for self-coaching in establishing clear communication.

What Kind of Parent Will You Be?

Pregnancy gives couples a chance to physically and emotionally prepare to bring their baby into the world. It gives them time to paint the nursery, purchase supplies and adjust to becoming parents. As the nine months draw to a close, mothers- and fathers-to-be try on and start settling into their new roles.

Gradually, as the couple wholly accepts this new phase in their union, they are able to catch a glimpse of the road ahead. For many, the image is a familiar one. That is because most people begin preparing for parenthood long before conception. Even before they become involved in a serious relationship, most young adults start thinking about the type of parent they will be.

Three Parenting Styles

Parenthood is at once awe-inspiring and terrifying. If this dichotomy lingers, parents may begin doubting their abilities. They wonder if they are doing this right or that wrong. They question their every move and hope that their instincts are correct. Most of the time their instincts are correct; but since parenting is a work in progress, practical knowledge is both helpful as well as reassuring.

Due to the nature of the relationship, parents are in a position of authority. It is important that they adapt to this with as much grace and wisdom as possible. How you parent affects how your child views himself and the world. While it is necessary to offer children guidance, they will not thrive in either a controlled or an unstructured environment. Extremes in parenting, such as the ones described below, leave children doubting and unprepared for life. The most successful parents learn balance. They lend a guiding hand as their children walk the path of youthful exploration.

The Authoritative Parent

An authoritative parent is one who controls every facet of his or her child's life. Children are given rules and expected to follow them to the letter with no deviations. Children who grow up under the guidance of this type of parent are often repressed and unsure of themselves. They have trouble with assertiveness, decision making, social skills, and self-esteem.

The Permissive Parent

At the other end of the parenting spectrum is the permissive parent. Opposing their authoritative counterparts, these parents give children complete control of their own upbringing. They do not establish rules or guidelines, therefore children of permissive parents never fully understand behavioral consequences. They do, however, learn the art of manipulation. Children who grow up with permissive parents often dictate family life and are well aware of how to get what they want. In the rush to make sure their children have a good life, permissive parents fail to teach them accountability and coach them in the behaviors that will help them succeed in life.

The Vigilant Parent

Vigilant parents are too protective of their children. While permissive parents lead a misguided quest for childhood happiness, vigilant parents do the same in the name of safety and well-being. They are the parents who rush to their child after every fall and scrape. They refuse to let their child play with other children because he might get sick or allow him to go swimming for fear he will drown. They view their role as one of vigilant protector, but at what cost? Children who have been sheltered by vigilant parents are often unable to cope with the stress of life or the reality of being an adult. They have had no practice weathering the rough patches and stress that are a part of every life.

After reviewing the three types of parenting styles that you do not want to assume, it is time to consider what type of parent you might be. Although, you may not want to wholly adopt any one of these parenting styles, raising children is not an all or nothing proposition. Your individual style will be a combination of bits and pieces. You will borrow from parents you respect, practice things you learn, and rely on skills you intuitively know.

We Parent the Way We Were Parented

As you reflect on the different parenting styles, you may feel nostalgic for your own childhood or for the childhood you wish you had lived. This may be because you recognize the parenting style you grew up with. The single most important influence on your parenting style will be the way you were parented. The methods your mother and father used and the words they spoke will come to you as naturally as breathing. Unfortunately, this can create an internal conflict if you experienced a damaging or unpleasant childhood.

Before you have children, it can be helpful to examine your own childhood. If you believe your upbringing was good and your parents were fair, the chances are that you will emulate their behavior. But if you did not have a good childhood and your parents employed stringent or hurtful methods, chances are you will still emulate them. That is, unless you make a concerted effort through self-coaching strategies and your personal success plan to deviate from the patterns of your childhood. This is possible through following many of the growth steps that I provide for you in this book. Remember to revise and write down your goals as you come to see more precisely what you want to achieve as a new parent. You will see the transformation as you take the action steps you designed. Self-coaching is a remarkable process which puts you in the driver's seat of making appropriate choices for the direction of your parenting skills.

If your parents spanked you for spilling your milk at the dinner table, do not be surprised when you instinctively want to raise your hand in the same future situation. Even though you are adamantly opposed to violence of any type, especially towards children, this reaction is ingrained like a habit. It is what you know because it is what you experienced.

During the most stressful parenting moments we all have a tendency to rely on what comes to us naturally from our past. Fortunately, we do not have to stay there.

For new parents who potentially face these types of situations, there are two things you must know. First, your parents did the best they knew how and so will you. Second, it is possible to change any type of pattern you have carried with you from childhood. First you must acknowledge it, and then you must have a plan in place to deal with it. You are designing this plan as you move through the suggestions in this book.

Use the exercise on the facing page to examine how you were parented. Record your answers in your journal and review them with your mate. Together you can use this information to acknowledge potential trouble spots and devise a parenting strategy for your future family.

Exercise: The Way You Were Parented

We all tend to parent as we were parented. For some people, it may be important that you make changes to the methods your mother and father used. In this exercise, complete the statements as they apply to your family of origin. Answer each question to the best of your ability to remember. Record your answers in a journal or on a separate sheet of paper.

1. In my family, the children were
2. In my family, my mother was the _____ and my father was the ____.
3. In my family, we __________________ together.
4. In my family, birthdays were
5. In my family, the children were punished
6. In my family, my parents never
7. In my family, discipline was
8. In my family, we showed love by
9. In my family, my parents always
10. In my family, the rules were

Review

Take a look at your responses. Take the positive aspects and place them in one column on a page in your journal. Next, look at the negative aspects and change each of them into a positive affirmation of how you would like to parent your child. Now make a list of the positive parenting statements that you will incorporate into your parenting plan. Use these affirmations daily as they will make a great difference in your ability to project positivity, harness any doubts and fears and help your mind focus on your desires as a new parent.

Sample Positive Affirmations:

I will speak to my child in a calm tone of voice.
I understand that my child is innocent and growing in wisdom.
I will take ten deep breaths to reduce an emotional charge.
I will connect with my child in the heart.

Your Image of Yourself as a Parent

Long before you have children, your mind recognizes the parent in you. Countless research studies show that all men and women carry with them an image of themselves as parents. This perception is a combination of a number of influences, which can include your parents, parental figures in your acquaintance, media portrayals and cultural expectations.

Your first and most lasting parental image is that of your mother and father. Their actions have the most influence on your perception of the ideal parent. If your relationship with your parents is good and your childhood was pleasant, chances are you will envision yourself in a similar role as nurturing parent. If the opposite is true, you may imagine yourself as being very different from the mother or father you grew up with. In addition to your parents of origin, other influential figures can shape your parenting self-image. Any person you identify as a parent figure can affect your concept of parenthood. This includes relatives, friends of the family, and parents of friends and neighbors.

Another entity that impacts your parenting self-image is the media. Media figures are often as influential as the aunt who bakes her children cookies everyday or the neighbor who coaches the soccer team. You may envision yourself doling out wisdom with compassion and authority in the style of *Father Knows Best* or may be unable to imagine yourself as a beer guzzling but lovable father like Homer Simpson.

In addition to these influences, current cultural mores also play a key role in how you imagine yourself as a parent. This is especially true for women. In the 1950s, there was no such thing as a stay-at-home mother by choice. At that time, women were expected to maintain the home and raise the children. It was not a choice; it was a woman's role in society. Therefore, it should come as no surprise that this cultural expectation worked its way into the parental self-images of the period.

As a whole, modern women have experienced many cultural changes, which have in turn affected the concept of parenthood. Before 1950, it was rare for a woman to voice career aspirations. But only forty short years later, women were being encouraged to "have it all"—career, home, husband, and children. In this relatively short period of time, women's role in the family and society underwent drastic changes that have turned parenthood into a partnership of teamwork and forever altered the face of the modern family.

One of the most noted changes of our time presents itself as less of a change and more of a choice. Today, women are given the choice of being a working or a stay-at-home parent. This decision is no longer a culturally imposed assumption nor is the stay-at-home parent always the mother. Even though economics dictate that most families have two working parents, many women and men choose to stay home once they bring children into the world.

Exercise: Parenting Self-Image

Before becoming parents, each of us envisions the type of parent we hope to be. This is your parenting self-image. Before you have children, this image will not have a constant mental presence, but it is valid and important to your new role. Take a moment to reflect on what type of parent you believe you will be. Find a quiet place where you can close your eyes and relax. Focus on the child you are expecting now or on the ones you hope to have in the future. Allow your mind to float between your current state and the parent you will soon be. What changes do you see? Do you look the same? Act the same? How do you hold your baby? Are you smiling? Is your child smiling?

I suggest that you allow your imagination to explore and answer any questions that come to you in this relaxed state. Encourage imagery and take note of any feelings or actions. When you come out of your relaxation, record your reactions to this exercise by listing them in your journal. Next, share them with your mate. Your impression of yourself in the exercise is yet another piece of the parent you will eventually become.

I ask you to record these impressions and tuck them away for now, and then I will ask you to revisit the type of parent you desire to be in Chapter Thirteen. The eight secrets to unlocking the keys of successful new parenting may enhance and shape your image of yourself as a new parent.

Defining Your Self as a Parent

You have considered how you were parented, the characteristics of several parenting styles, and your parenting self-image. Now it is time to put it all together and start to shape or define a parenting role for you, knowing that it will expand and re-form itself as you move through the eight secrets.

The moment your child is born, both you and your life story change. Each of us has a story that begins with our birth and constantly evolves and grows with us. This story is the seed of your being and the root of your self-esteem. At this point, your story is about to change significantly. In other words, your parenting story is about to begin.

As you embark on this new phase in your life, it is important for you to record your impressions. Begin writing your parenting story in whatever form with which you are comfortable: journal, essay, or letter. Start with your definition of yourself as a parent. Review the last three exercises and combine your discoveries to define yourself as a parent.

Your definition can serve as a roadmap on the way to parenthood. Be sure to retain your records, keeping these initial impressions, hopes, and dreams to review over the years as you and your parenting style change. It is always wonderful to know where you started so you can measure how much you have grown.

Secrets for New Parents

As a pregnant couple, you have many resources when it comes to advice about breastfeeding and diaper changing. But when you need encouragement and reassurance, most of you will turn to your mate. That is why your relationship should be a priority. It will sustain you during your pregnancy and the early days of parenthood. This partnership will be what keeps you on track and your family strong.

In the earlier chapters, you learned how to assess your individual situations to gauge your likelihood for parenting success. The same process can be used to assess the probability of success in your relationships. Identify the characteristics you share as a couple that will serve you well as parents. Also pinpoint those that need improvement. Once again, the form of your goals may change through the next seven chapters. This process can be highly beneficial when you undertake a significant transition such as the one from couple to family. In the following chapters, we will explore the eight secrets to successful parenting.

Eight Secrets for New Parents to Master

I use the word secrets to describe basic foundation traits that all new parents need to maintain mental, emotional, and physical health. Better than that, these foundational traits translate into concrete, real-life coaching skills that you can practice now in your partnership.

Research has demonstrated that a depressed mom is more likely to have a depressed toddler. An angry father may demonstrate such behavioral patterns for his child to model. To change these patterns now is a golden opportunity to be a successful person, and moreover, an outstanding parent. Here are the 8 secrets that every new parent should know, and I will walk you through every step on your journey to success.

Secret One: Healthy Self-Esteem

Long-standing research in education and psychology consistently has correlated healthy levels of self-esteem to success and leadership. Healthy self-esteem gives you the edge as a successful, nurturing parent in that you will find yourself with more confidence and willingness to grow with your mate.

Secret Two: Open Communication

A fundamental truth about relationships is that your intimacy is founded upon your ability to speak with each other and trust what you hear. Communication consists of speaking a clear message and also listening with attention. It is true that if you don't speak and listen clearly with each other, then your children are likely to get mixed messages about what you expect from them. How lucky you are that you have started on your personal growth journeys with each other, using your self-coaching skills.

Secret Three: Solving Problems and Resolving Conflict

Believe it or not the majority of people do not know how to solve a problem. A problem requires that someone observe the situation, assess the dynamics, review the resources and then think through viable solutions. For example, if you knew ahead of time that you would be breastfeeding your newborn, then you would anticipate any problems you might encounter and then educate yourself on the solutions. You might keep a reference book on breastfeeding nearby for those small emergency questions. It is possible to anticipate the major problems of being a new parent and educate yourself to solve the problem before it happens.

Secret Four: Managing Stress

If you do encounter problems or conflicts, there is no reason that you have to panic or be fearful that you cannot handle it. Through the fourth secret, you will learn to identify your stressors as well as your reaction patterns to stress. Once you know which behaviors are unproductive for you or causes you distress, you can change them.

Secret Five: Building Resilience

Building resilience is probably one of the more important secrets because of its ability to impact your entire life significantly. Daily exercises for physical health, mental health and emotional fitness are plentiful in this chapter. You will benefit from coaching yourself in resilience right away because it serves you best in the first two months your child is home.

Secret Six: Trusting Your Intuition

I have interviewed many parents in my private practice, workshops and seminars whose children were under one year of age. When I asked them which secrets they thought were important for new parents, they rated trusting intuition as high. I believe that their responses were influenced by their status as new parents because they had to make decisions and solve problems quickly. They were accustomed to going with their gut level feeling. It often turned out to be right.

Also when you receive advice about parenting from well-intended family members, sometimes it is most important that you learn to trust your own feelings about the situation. When you do so, you'll arrive at an answer that stems from your confidence rather than another's advice.

Secret Seven: Caring and Patience

The qualities of patience and caring will not appear automatically when your child is born, but these two qualities are profound in their effects upon your relationships. If you don't give or receive enough patience and caring in your relationship, then start practicing now by building loving habits that will be passed on to your child.

Secret Eight: Flexibility

When your child comes home, time disappears. You enter an environment of meeting the needs of your child on her schedule, and time seems to go away for a while. Rather than set your life by the clock, you learn to be fluid in the dance with your child and each other. You want to enjoy this auspicious dance, as it happens only once. The dance will bring you the flexibility to adjust to your new relationships.

Exercise: Do you know the secret?

Use the following exercise to explore how you and your mate rate as a couple when it comes to the eight secrets of successful new parents. On a scale of one to eight, with one being the lowest and eight being the highest, rate how prepared you feel in each area. Then, use the results to formulate a success plan that incorporates the eight secrets for new parents into your life.

Self-Esteem	1	2	3	4	5	6	7	8
Intuition	1	2	3	4	5	6	7	8
Communication	1	2	3	4	5	6	7	8
Patience	1	2	3	4	5	6	7	8
Conflict Resolution	1	2	3	4	5	6	7	8
Stress Management	1	2	3	4	5	6	7	8
Flexibility	1	2	3	4	5	6	7	8
Resiliency	1	2	3	4	5	6	7	8

Summary

In this chapter, you learned how to use your self-coaching skills to evaluate relationships prior to transitioning into parenthood. You also learned that this transition is not instant, but one that develops over time and runs the course of a physical pregnancy. This transition is divided into three stages—Acceptance, Separation, and Exploration. At each stage, expectant parents become increasingly aware of their growing child and their role as parent. When preparing for parenthood, use your self-coaching tools to identify the changes you and your mate wish to make individually and as a couple. Find out which of the eight secrets for new parents you already possess; then create and implement a success plan to help you embrace the others.

Wallet Card

Below, you will find some simple coaching points to remember. Read the points from the end of each chapter, then cut each card out from the back of the book and keep it with you to remind you of your goals.

- I trust my intuition.
- I communicate openly and listen attentively.
- I act with patience and nurture with care.
- I prepare myself through positivity for new parenting roles.

CHAPTER SIX

The First Secret

Self-Esteem

CHAPTER OBJECTIVES

- Assess your self-esteem.
- Understand your self-image and know your value and worth.
- Learn self-esteem affirmations.
- Know how self-esteem can support changes as new parents.
- Learn to manage self-esteem in unfamiliar territory.
- Practice self-coaching tips for personal esteem and in support of your mate.

You cannot be lonely if you like the person you're alone with.

—Dr. Wayne Dyer

To establish true self-esteem we must concentrate on our successes and forget about the failures and the negatives in our lives.

—Denis Waitley

In Chapter One, you learned that to know yourself well is the first, crucial step in your success plan. To know you in the deepest sense includes an exploration into the concept of self-esteem, especially as it relates to preparing for parenting. In Chapters Two through Four, you completed assessments of your strengths and skills to clarify your goals and define action steps. In this chapter, you will learn how self-esteem is the critical foundation upon which all other success factors are built.

Many Faces of Self-Esteem

Self-esteem is how you value yourself. You have lived with yourself 24 hours a day all of your life. Truly, given the time and energy that you invest in your self-coaching program, you will know yourself inside and out, and your self-esteem will be your strong foundation.

For example, part of self-esteem is an image of yourself formed in childhood that you hold in your head. As you matured, the image changed based upon your interactions with people and the influences of your environment.

Feelings that you have about yourself are the second part of self-esteem. You have felt comfort as well as discomfort based upon your self-image. You have felt both highs and lows throughout your lifetime. You learned how to feel good about yourself when you were in familiar territory, accomplished your goals, won prizes for your creativity or received praise for your actions. You felt low when in a state of fear, feeling rejection or criticism.

High and low feelings shift quickly. For example, on a summer day when a brother takes his little sister hiking over boulders, pretending to be mountain climbing, the little sister is exhilarated by achieving this goal. When she bursts into the kitchen to tell her mother the exciting news, she finds her mother scowling and shushing her because mom is on the telephone. Little sister's feeling of elation deflates quickly and her self-esteem is low for a while.

From this example, you can see that self-esteem is not a *fixed* image or feeling as you grow up. It constantly shifts as you move throughout your life. As an adult, however, you settle into a comfortable image that works for you. The self-image that you adopt as an adult will include what you think you look like physically, how your personality comes across to others, what kind of person you think you are and how much you like yourself or you think others like you. You may compare yourself to others and be critical or accept yourself in your uniqueness and be empowered.

Self-Esteem Assessment

Exercise: Self-Esteem Questions

Please answer yes or no to the following questions. When you ask yourself these questions, don't think too hard about the answers. You receive a more natural answer when you let the response jump into your mind from a stream of consciousness. Remember to keep a journal of your answers as you go through this book because it will empower your personal coaching plan for success.

1. Do I think I am a worthwhile person? Y N
2. Can I laugh at myself? Y N
3. Can I see my value as a mate, professional or friend? Y N
4. Do I have respect for myself? Y N
5. Can I see my image in the mirror and be pleased? Y N
6. Overall, do I feel like I am successful? Y N
7. I can love and support myself no matter what happens around me? Y N
8. Can I be resourceful when necessary? Y N
9. Can I like myself even when I feel rejected by others? Y N
10. Do I value self-growth and learning? Y N
11. Do I have or can I develop the personal qualities to live a successful life? Y N

Evaluation

The questions serve as your check-in about self-esteem. When you look at your answers, you will see if you need a reminder to boost your esteem, or if your esteem is already healthy and strongly supporting your life.

The yes and no answers force you to review your perceptions of values, self-respect, humor and other attitudes which are part of healthy self-esteem. The more questions that you marked with a YES response, the healthier is your esteem. If you responded to half or more of the questions with NO, then these are self-esteem traits that need improvement. Establish goals to build your esteem in these areas of improvement and also create affirmations for yourself. Here are some examples.

Area of Change One: The way I feel about myself in the mirror.

Goal: I will have a consultation with a makeover artist. I will consider two suggestions to improve my appearance and make these happen!

Positive Affirmation: I like what I see and I love who I am!

Area of Change Two: Feel that I am successful.

Goal: I will interview three solid, successful people I admire and find their definitions of success. I will choose three common success traits and will develop those traits within myself.

Positive Affirmation: I am a phenomenally successful person that others admire.

Self-Coaching Good Thoughts

These are aspects of your life that are great and do not need improvement. By focusing on what is right about yourself, you feel better about your skills and accomplishments to date. They become the basis for your continued progress. When you build upon what is right, you enable further growth. It is everyone's inner nature to want to be better and grow. One way to do that is through the use of positive language and thought. Below are some statements that affirm your worth and increase esteem. I suggest that you read these several times a day to remind your inner voice that this is your new language. Feel free to add others from the above exercise to affirm and empower yourself.

1. I am aware of my strengths, and I like them.
2. I feel secure within myself.
3. I appreciate other's gifts and talents, as I do my own.
4. I compare myself to no one else as I am whole unto myself.
5. I have good judgment in my professional life.
6. I like be alone with myself and enjoy my personal time.
7. I stay interested in and love learning.
8. I influence others positively and kindly.
9. I help others compassionately.
10. My judgment is sound.

Self-Esteem and Unfamiliar Territory

We all feel best about ourselves when we are in familiar territory. Yet with practice and interest, even the unfamiliar situations can become comfortable. For example, you may be a top-notch professional in your field, feeling great about how you look and what you accomplish. You have vibrant energy and move through your day with a smile for everyone. You are in familiar territory in your profession and your healthy self-worth shines through.

What happens when you enter unfamiliar territory like having your first child? New parenting situations may test your feelings of self-worth. Remember though, it is only unfamiliar to you and not a situation in which you are incompetent or unable to excel.

Julie, aged thirty-three, had planned for her first child for two years. Julie and her husband, Lee, felt educated, prepared, and enthusiastic for their son's arrival. They bubbled with pride when they brought Cash home to meet his grandparents who were helping out.

After two weeks, Julie gave me a call for a private consultation because she felt she was losing her identity. "Dr. Sharon, I have infinite patience for my son finding his own schedule for breastfeeding and sleeping. I don't mind the crazy hours of no sleep. What I am having trouble with is I don't know who I am anymore."

"Julie, explain that to me."

"I am not the Human Resources Coach any more. I know I am Cash's mom, but I don't feel that deep bond that the books talk about yet. I don't know if I can handle all of this losing my identity as a professional and being absorbed solely into Cash's life. Won't I go nuts?"

Like most new parents, Julie felt she had plummeted down the rabbit's hole like Alice in Wonderland. She didn't know where she was. The new adventure of parenthood was a foreign world of sleep deprivation, crazy feeding schedules, fatigue, and the lingering stress of the entire delivery process. Sounds like the scene in a fiction novel where the heroine is experiencing brainwashing, doesn't it?

The confusion as to one's personal identity is normal, and Julie felt much better as a result of talking to another person about it. She missed the interaction with her peers and now found another adult voice that was supportive and informative. She also needed to understand that all new moms feel this way, and the vast majority of new moms adjust within three to five months.

Julie learned to stop placing idealistic expectations on herself and was able to take one day at a time. Over time and through trial-and-error interactions with her child and her husband, Julia will become more familiar with the territory to develop self-confidence and feel more worthy in her role as Mom.

Self-Esteem and New Parenting

Nathaniel Brandon, Ph.D., is an original founder of the National Association for Self-Esteem. He said that healthy self-esteem is "the experience of being capable of meeting life's challenges and being worthy of happiness."[1]

Even if Julie felt like she had an identity crisis as a new mom in the first month, she was confident and willing to personally coach herself to rise through the challenges that greeted her as the mother of a newborn.

When preparing for being a new parent and educating yourself as to the challenges that await you, it is important for you to understand how certain factors will impact your new role.

- Socially, your relationships move from being a tight-knit couple with friends who have children or no children to being a family unit. Your prior life of being a couple now takes the back seat to that of being the family. Socially, you'll find yourself desiring a mom's support group, a conversation with other dads, or confirmation from others in your age range who have shared similar sleepless nights.
- Cultural expectations change for new parents. You'll be expected to stay home and not party as much as you had. Grandparents will expect to assist and offer support where they can. You'll need a babysitter so the two of you can have needed time for yourselves. You'll seek out restaurants for families and not for a couple's romantic meal.
- Interpersonal changes occur that involve your physical health and stress levels, intimacy in sexuality, communication, and even the opportunity of sharing meals together if one of you works and one stays home to parent.
- All these changes are compounded into one small slice of nine months during which you are expected to adjust physically, emotionally, mentally, spiritually, and socially.
- You can easily see why self-coaching becomes a savvy model for developing your skills as a person of value both during pregnancy as well as after delivery.

Significance of Self-Esteem

Nathaniel Branden also stated that, "There is overwhelming evidence, including scientific research findings, that the higher the level of an individual's self-esteem, the more likely that he or she will treat others with respect, kindness, and generosity."[2]

It pays to coach yourself to stronger self-worth as you prepare for parenting. You are in training and building your strength. Your inner strength and resilience as a new parent is required and highly advantageous to you. In turn, your self-esteem is boosted.

Healthy self-esteem correlates to a stronger sense of personal control. So just at the time of your life when you may feel that you are not in control, your inner strength can shine through. The healthiest person today is a person who feels good about her diet, exercise and health, attitude and activities, making her less susceptible to distress.

A strong sense of esteem is important for new parenting for two more reasons.

1. In unfamiliar territory, you will tend to act consistently with respect to your belief about yourself. There is an innate trust you can feel in healthy esteem that brings you through the toughest times. It is called resilience and is the fifth secret in Chapter 10. If you feel you'll be a great parent, you *will be* despite the ups and downs that occur with normal mood swings. Your core belief in yourself is your inner strength that will sustain you through the now-and-then blues. If you are committed to keeping the lines of communication open with your mate, then you will. If you believe that you are secure enough within yourself to dive into all of the new experiences that parenting brings, then you will be.
2. Your view of the world around you is filtered through your sense of self-worth. When preparing to be new parents, you and your mate must hold each other in high regard and appreciation. Your vision of how your family develops will come from how you value each other and appreciate each of your roles in the parenting process.

Now that you understand more about self-esteem and its importance to this new phase of your lives, let's move on to preparing for the positive changes ahead.

Self-Esteem Coaching for New Parents

- You are accountable for your feelings. When tired or overwhelmed, it is easy to take out feelings of ill will on your mate. Signs of ill will might be irritability, fatigue, being snappy, or using biting words.

> **Tip:** Remember this phrase, "Please don't take me personally."

- High self-esteem does not equate to healthy self-esteem. Sometimes people with high self-esteem are overly confident, try too hard or are arrogant. Healthy esteem looks at the reality of life and deals with it one day at a time.

> **Tip:** Healthy self-esteem is being aware of your faults and improving each day in a new way. Remember this phrase, "I improve today in a new way."

- Healthy self-esteem does not require perfectionism. Rather, you realize that you and everyone else will make mistakes. You don't regret them. Instead, utilize them as feedback so you can make required corrections. In the face of errors, you still find self-value.

> **Tip:** Remember this phrase, "I value myself today in every way."

- Healthy self-esteem doesn't leave room for blame or self-pity, yet accepts feelings as real and valid.

Tip: Remember this phrase, "I accept my feelings and don't need a pity party."

- Healthy self-esteem chooses to stretch, to learn, and to grow. On those days of feeling like you've been stretched on a rack, can you still laugh with your mate and hug each other through it all?

Tip: Remember this phrase, "I always learn from my experiences, even the hardest ones."

- Healthy self-esteem ensures that you take care of yourself first so you also have the energy and focus to take care of your mate and your other family members.

Tip: Each day I will check in with myself to ensure that my needs are taken care of, and then check with my mate to see how I can help, if needed.

Nurturing Self-Esteem in Each Other

Self-Coaching Skill: Appreciate Your Mate

To be a nurturing parent to your expected child starts with being nurturing in your relationship to yourself and your mate. The beginning of this chapter stated that self-esteem was the foundation of all success traits and qualities. A healthy sense of worth is a quality of your character that you demonstrate through adopting positive attitudes and affirming behaviors. Being able to nurture another person, specifically your mate, requires self-confidence and a stronger sense of personal satisfaction.

Abraham Maslow, a humanistic psychologist, developed a theory of a hierarchy of human needs that every person passes through on their way to self-realization. Self-esteem is a step on the hierarchy, and Maslow explained two kinds of esteem that every person needs. The first is the need for self-respect, and the second is respect from others.

- Self-respect includes expertise, confidence, accomplishment, independence, and freedom.
- Respect from others entails recognition, acceptance, and appreciation.

This respect and appreciation are the qualities you extend to your mate. It is good practice to make a concerted effort at appreciation and respect for your mate before the baby arrives. The effort spent in practicing appreciation in times of less stress will help you to make respect a habit in your lives. Then these qualities come more naturally when you are busily in the midst of caring for your baby.

Self-Coaching Skill: Practice Extending Yourself

If you are not comfortable with yourself, you won't often feel comfortable extending yourself for another person. Being comfortable with yourself, you will more easily go the extra mile in order to help your mate adjust to the changing times. In his book *The Road Less Traveled*, the author, M. Scott Peck, said that "Love is extending yourself for another's growth."

Extending yourself might be biting your tongue instead of lashing out when you are tired. It might be a heart-to-heart conversation about a difficult topic that you and your mate need to have. Are there issues you need to clear up as a couple before bringing a child into your family? Extending yourself as a mate, and later as a parent, means that you may do something that initially seems difficult for you, but you know that dealing with it will help both of you.

Self-Coaching Skill: Focus and Practice with Each Other

What new skills do you need to practice as a new parent? Is there an attitude that you want to rehearse before jumping into a time compression of nine months when time flies and you are absorbed in the life of your child? Focus your attention on your mate. Before each of you leaves for the day, pool your lists of tasks and see how you can help each other accomplish them. Whoever comes home earlier in the evening from work, call first and offer to run those last minute errands? Don't feel like cooking? Then plan a surprise meal, delivered to your door. Yes, even pizza looks great some nights. You are becoming a team, each working for the benefit of the other and the team.

Through the practice of focusing on each other's needs and checking in with each other for task fulfillment, you are building the bridges of teamwork. You are practicing cooperation now, establishing the habit as a couple. As a result, you are much more likely to be steadfast and stable mates, ready to welcome your child into a healthy family atmosphere!

My (Our) Plan for Change

Record your answers in your journal or on a separate sheet of paper.

1. Change I would like to make

Goal: What do I see as the result of my change?

Action Steps: Taking one step at a time, how will I accomplish my goal?

Positive Affirmations (to be repeated daily)

2. Change I would like to make

Goal: What do I see as the result of my change?

Action Steps: Taking one step at a time, how will I accomplish my goal?

Positive Affirmations (to be repeated daily)

Summary

Self-esteem consists of how you see yourself and how you feel about yourself. Your perceptions can include your physical appearance, your social skills, how you think others view you and any comparisons that you make between yourself and others.

Self-esteem is a critical foundation for successful new parents, and this chapter has covered ways to build self-esteem through coaching tips before your child arrives. Practicing self-esteem before birthing makes self-esteem a habit when your new child comes home. Self-coaching tips include

- Being accountable for your feelings
- Being willing to make mistakes, allowing others their mistakes and learning together
- Choosing to grow and stretch beyond comfort levels
- Accepting and validating moods and feelings without blame
- Appreciating your mate
- Extending yourself
- Focus and practice with your mate

Wallet Card

Below, you will find some simple coaching points to remember. Cut each card out from the back of the book and keep it with you to remind you of your goals.

- I am accountable for my feelings.
- I stretch and grow beyond my comfort zone.
- I value myself and appreciate my mate.
- I practice self-esteem now to have healthy self-worth when my child arrives.

CHAPTER SEVEN

The Second Secret

Effective Communication

CHAPTER OBJECTIVES

- Distinguish between positive and negative communication practices.
- Assess your current communication practices with your mate.
- Learn the nine traits of effective communicators.
- Apply effective communication skills in your partnership and other relationships.

Tell me and I'll forget. Show me and I'll remember.
Involve me and I'll understand.

—Confucius

Every good relationship is built on solid communication. In your partnership and for your success plan for new parents, I advise you to make clear and concise communication your top priority. Communication skills, whether they are positive or negative, are a defining factor in every relationship. Negative communication skills, such as not listening or monopolizing conversations, lead to a sense of disrespect and futility. On the other hand, practicing healthy communication helps mates realize and maintain a productive and fulfilling relationship.

Communication enables you to be a more effective person. In this chapter, you will learn to distinguish between positive and negative communication practices. You and your mate will assess your current communication practices, and identify the good and not so good skills that define your relationship. You will also learn the nine traits that all effective communicators have in common and how you can use these traits to strengthen your relationship.

Being an Effective Communicator

Within each of us is the power to be either positive or negative. This is true in all aspects of our lives including communication. Positive communicators approach problems and solutions with an eye towards being helpful and supportive. They put their all into resolving conflict and do not expect their mates to speculate on the source of their happiness or hurt. Positive communicators know mind reading is a rare skill, and to rely on telepathy is both foolish and counterproductive. Instead, they use a clear voice to concisely and honestly speak with their mates.

Negative communicators, on the other hand, have a tendency to lecture, monopolize and manipulate conversations. This type of behavior is often interpreted as disrespectful and makes their mates feel belittled and insignificant. When they do give others the chance to speak, many times instead of listening, they go inside their own heads to formulate rebuttals. These people are often seen as more interested in being right than in promoting harmony in their relationships and self-esteem in their mates.

Like everything else you have learned thus far, it is important that new and prospective parents have solid communication skills. In the previous chapter, you read how positive self-esteem, a feeling of confidence, is an important foundation upon which to build the subsequent skills.

Blocks to Effective Communication

Here are the four biggest blocks to effective communication with your mate, and you can see how these blocks are related to healthy or unhealthy self-esteem.

Communication Block One: "I need to be right."

- Unhealthy self-esteem: *I'm right about this. I know I am. I don't want to lose face here I am invested in being right.*
- Healthy self-esteem: *I would rather be in love than be right. If his need is that strong, then let him be right. I'd would rather listen and observe.*

Communication Block Two: "I am afraid."

- Unhealthy self-esteem: *If I tell her she'll be mad at me. I cannot hurt his feelings by telling him the truth.*
- Healthy self-esteem: *The truth may hurt on this subject, but let's talk this through. We are mature enough to face this issue. We'll get over hurt feelings, but would we get over dishonesty?*

Communication Block Three: "I can't face you. I am running away."

- Unhealthy self-esteem*: I cannot stand confrontation. I'd rather die than face him. She nags at me all the time. I can't stand her grating voice. I have to walk away, man.*
- Healthy self-esteem: *We can face each other. We will remain present. This challenge will help us grow and learn together.*

Communication Block Four: "I hear you, but I don't get it. I need to clear up her problems; she just doesn't understand. He never listens; he just projects his stuff all over me."

- Unhealthy self-esteem: *She can talk all she wants, but she never says anything. He doesn't get it. It seems like he is listening, then he goes off on a tangent.*
- Healthy self-esteem: *We listen to each other respectfully. We are not thinking about our own agendas. We listen to connect and truly hear each other.*

If you fell into one or two of these categories, don't feel bad. No one grows up with perfect communication that they modeled from their perfect parents, who were our first models of communication. Throughout your growing up, you may have developed a fear of confrontation because loud voices and screaming upset you. Perhaps you were told that children should be seen but not heard. And if you were never heard, then you may have the need to prove yourself right. The good news is that we can learn to become skilled communicators through our self-coaching program.

Effective Positive Communication

How well you communicate has a direct effect on the success of your relationship. Therefore, improving your communication skills can have an impact on your performance as a couple and as parents. If you are persistent in your self-coaching practices, you can only grow and improve in this area. I have provided the necessary skill-building steps for you.

For many people, new parenting is a substantial adjustment. It takes a great deal of energy and focus to make the transition from a relationship as mates to parents. In addition, learning how to communicate effectively now can make you a positive role model later. As with most behavior, children learn how to communicate from their parents. Consequently, if you and your mate establish effective communication before you become parents, it will be easier to teach your children how to use these skills to get the most out of their lives.

People who can explain and listen effectively are highly influential and well respected. The key to being a good communicator is *how* you communicate, not necessarily the content of *what* you say.

Coaching Tips for Effective Communication

If you are having problems in the communication arena, the following list of specific self-coaching tips has proven to be helpful for others and can alert you to communication opportunities.

1. Staying focused in your communication is keeping your eye on your audience and your mind on your topic.
2. Have a conversation rather than give a lecture or deliver a monologue. A genuine conversation flows from you easily, like having a cup of coffee with a friend.
3. Speak clearly in words that are inviting and engaging, not with words that produce stumbling blocks or barriers. For example, use simple language and not clichés or jargon. A journalist writes in simple words and phrases for the average newspaper reader, basically for an eighth grade reading level.
4. The human mind thinks in images and pictures. Paint pictures with your words. Use metaphors or tell a story to get your point across.
5. Stay in the present tense with your conversation. Wandering to the past isn't necessary.

(Text continues on page 131.)

Exercise: Practice Positive Communication

The ability to choose the good over the bad is a characteristic shared by positive people. The same goes for positive communicators. The following scenarios in this exercise have three parts:

- The rule of positive communication,
- A story that exemplifies a negative approach to typical communication, and
- A section that says, "Your Turn: Turn this negative situation into one of positive communication."

As you read each story of how communication is used negatively, envision yourself in the role of communicator. How would you turn each negative approach into a positive one? I advise you to write your answers in your journal so you can review the skills you want to include in your self-coaching plan.

There are nine examples. I have provided the positive communication examples for you in the first two rules of positive communication. By following my examples of turning a negative situation into a positive one, you can do the same for rules 3 through 8.

1. Know the situation Before you become angry or offer your mate unsolicited advice, be sure you have all of the information. If you speak or act before you know all there is to know about the situation at hand, you risk wasting time and unnecessarily offending your mate.

Christina was jolted awake by the sound of something breaking. She rushed from bed into the living room where her husband, Ed, was sweeping up what was left of her favorite flower vase. Anger rose inside of her and tears filled her eyes. Her great aunt Cecilia had given her that vase when she graduated from college. She couldn't help but yell at him for being so clumsy and not looking where he was going. She was so mad and blamed him for her loss. It wasn't until she saw the confused look on his face that she stopped. "I know I was the one that wanted the puppy," said Ed. "But you agreed and you can't blame me every time he messes something up. That is what puppies do. He will grow out of it and I am sure he didn't mean to knock the end table over and break your vase." With that he turned his back on her and his shoulders slumped as he finished sweeping up the glass.

Your Turn Turn this negative approach into a positive communication. When Christina rushed into the room and saw Ed sweeping up the vase her Aunt Cecilia had given her; she wanted to yell at him through her tears. However, when she saw the confused look on his face, she stopped herself and asked,

"The puppy did it, didn't he?" Ed nodded his head and suggested that Christina join him for a cup of tea to discuss how to train the puppy for better discipline or else remove valuable objects from the puppy's environment.

Another way to handle the above scenario is for Christine to apologize for yelling at Ed and to offer him a hug and help in cleaning up.

2. Act on fact, not opinion All of us have opinions on everything. Therefore, it is extremely important that you be able to separate fact from opinion in your communication. Opinion is how you feel about something. It is influenced by a number of outside factors, unlike simple facts. When dealing with others it is best to operate on fact as much as possible since the reality of a situation does not change according to individual preferences.

For his birthday Larry wanted to try a new Indian restaurant that just opened downtown. His girlfriend, Ellen, would do anything to make sure he had a good birthday, except eat downtown. The last time she was downtown in the business district, a rat scurried across the road in front of her car. If she was seeing rats in broad daylight then every building must be infested. She had always heard that for every one rodent you saw there were twenty more just around the corner. It made her sick to think about how many would be in a restaurant where they had easy access to food. She ended up telling Larry she would be glad to make reservations at a restaurant in another part of town, but she could not eat in that rat-infested place.

Your Turn Turn this negative approach into a positive communication.
In order to help Ellen stop responding emotionally from an opinion not based on fact, Larry needs to have a heart-to-heart conversation with Ellen. He can point out her lack of logic in her thinking that "every building is rat-infested." He can also point out that she is letting her fear run amok by making inflations of one fact: a rat once ran in front of her car. The three steps he might follow are

A Getting her to agree that she won't go out to eat on his birthday because of her fear and opinion

B Asking if she is willing to recognize the real facts and have dinner with him.

C If she is willing, then make the dinner reservations immediately. If she is not willing, then Larry will have to choose whether or not to join Ellen at the restaurant of her choice.

3. Share the blame When talking with your mate about a problem or making a constructive suggestion, avoid using the word you. When a statement begins with you, it casts blame, which will put your mate on the defensive. Instead, offer to share responsibility for the situation. Replace you with the

Exercise continued on the following page

word we. For instance, if it is important for you to be punctual but your husband does not share your urgency, telling him that he is never on time solves nothing. Instead share the responsibility by offering to remind him fifteen minutes before you need to leave of the time. This takes the sting of accusation out of your statement and the blame off your mate's shoulders.

Marshall stormed out of the bathroom and screamed down the stairs. "Katie, you never pick your towel up after you take a shower," said Marshall. "I am getting really tired of cleaning up after you. I am your husband, not your maid." Katie was already late for work but she knew he was right. She didn't pick up her towel but she didn't always leave her things on the floor either. She hesitated before turning around and climbing in her car. She probably would have gone back inside if she didn't feel as if he was always blaming her for things she didn't do.

Your Turn Turn this negative approach into a positive communication.

4. Deal with it When faced with inappropriate behavior, you can handle the situation in a way that encourages the desired behavior without analyzing or embarrassing your mate. A solution-based approach that includes consequences is most effective.

She could not believe Dennis came home for lunch and left a sink full of dirty dishes. Ever since Marianne started working from home, she felt as if her husband, Dennis, took her for granted. He let all of the errands pile up and many times he did not do the chores he had always done. Just because she worked at home did not mean she had the time to deal with her work and his too. Marianne believed that since Dennis was raised by a stay-at-home mother, he pictured her in the same role and that was simply not the case. It wasn't the case now nor would it be the case when they had children of their own. When he got home from work, she was going to remind him she wasn't his mother.

Your Turn Turn this negative approach into a positive communication.

5. Strike a balance Most of us do not respond well to constant criticism. In addition to lowering our self-esteem, it makes us feel defeated and incapable. Therefore, it is important when offering your mate constructive criticism that you also offer praise. The two balance each other out. Praise makes criticism easier to accept, which in turn makes the situation easier to rectify.

When Stacy broke her leg, her husband, Evan, did not hesitate to assume her half of the household chores. He ran the vacuum cleaner, mopped the kitchen floor, and cleaned the bathrooms. He even brought her meals in bed! Unfortunately, he was also washing the dishes and he did not do as thorough a job as Stacy. One morning, after a particularly painful and restless night, Stacy picked up her toast only to find ketchup on the plate. "Can't you do anything," she screamed. "I am lying here and all I ask for is a clean plate." Visibly hurt, Evan took the plate to the kitchen and left for work without saying goodbye.

Your Turn Turn this negative approach into a positive communication.

6. Don't get personal We make personal observations about the habits of others, especially the ones that annoy us. There is no room for these observations when making criticisms or suggestions. Bringing them up in these types of conversations will only serve to alienate and perhaps hurt your mate.

Abby bites her fingernails when she is nervous and boy did she have something to be nervous about. She was offered a huge promotion at work and she was going to share her good news with her husband, Tom, over dinner. Unfortunately, her news was not all good. The promotion would involve a transfer and Abby knew this would not appeal to Tom. They thought they had finally settled down. They had worked hard to renovate their house and had even thought about starting a family. Abby loved all this about their life, but she had worked hard for this promotion. At dinner she was so nervous she could not even eat. She had chewed her nails to the quick. Finally, she blurted everything out and as she suspected Tom was very critical of the timing. "I can't believe after all this time, you get a promotion," said Tom. "I really thought we had built a home here. Even though it surprises me that you got anything done with your fingers in your mouth all the time.

Your Turn Turn this negative approach into a positive communication.

7. Choose your words Just as words can be powerful tools, they can be powerful weapons as well. Being mindful that what you say and how you say it can be the difference between constructive and destructive criticism. It can also be the difference between being hurtful and solving a problem.

Dick is a self-employed graphic designer who works out of his home. His wife, Sara, is an accountant. Of the two of them, Sara was definitely tidier. When he moved his office into the spare bedroom, he and Sara decided it would be on a trial basis to make sure it worked for both of them. He loved it, but gradually his work made its way out of the bedroom and into the rest of the house. He tried to keep it under control and some days he succeeded but others he did not. When he came home from his workout on

Exercise continued on the following page

Wednesday afternoon, he was greeted by a screaming Sara. "I can't take it any more," said Sara. "This constantly picking up after you is driving me crazy. I'm just not sure how much longer I can do this." When he heard this, Dick got scared. He wasn't sure if Sara was referring to his messy habits or their marriage.

Your Turn Turn this negative approach into a positive communication.

8. In general General or vague statements are counterproductive. Many times your mate may not know what you are talking about or how to respond in the conversation. It is important to be specific when offering criticism or making suggestions. Otherwise, your words may go in one ear and out the other.

Patty had no idea what she was supposed to do. She and her husband Wayne had started the day with an argument. The last thing he said before leaving was that she never made him feel special anymore. What was that supposed to mean? She had spent the entire day at work thinking over their five years together and still wasn't sure what he meant. Now, he would be home any minute and she wanted to do the right thing. She just wasn't sure what that was.

Your Turn Turn this negative approach into a positive communication.

9. Absolutely not Absolutes, like the words never and always, tend to be overlooked in conversation and rarely convey what you really mean. It may feel as if your mate never mows the yard or always spends too much at the grocery store, but the use of absolutes only opens the door for an unnecessary argument.

Dale was fuming by the time he reached the house. As usual, Elizabeth had not put gas in the car and with the broken fuel gauge he had no idea until he ran out. The entire walk home, all he could think about was how to best approach the situation. Instead of calling on the logical suggestions he formulated on the way home, when he saw his wife all he could do was scream. "You never put gas in the car and I am always the one to pay for your mistake."

Your Turn Turn this negative approach into a positive communication.

Communicating with Your Mate

The previous exercise reveals nine communication pitfalls all couples should be aware of. Hopefully, the act of changing the negative communication practices into positive ones has made you more cognizant and diligent of how to improve your personal skills. Unfortunately, for many people that will not be the case. As we are all well aware, it is easier to see and identify points of concern in others than it is in yourself. With that in mind, I think it is time to turn the tables and stretch into self-coaching skills.

Exercise: Turning the Communication Tables

For the next week, whenever you or your mate feels as if you are having problems communicating, use your journal and take note of the situation. Each of you needs to briefly describe the situation—what happened, what you were doing, what happened beforehand, and what happened afterwards.

Also, be sure to describe how you felt and your gut reaction to the miscommunication. At the end of the week, you and your mate will compare lists. How many situations are on both of your lists? Did you describe these situations in a similar manner? React to them similarly? Are these situations reoccurring? If so, what does that say about your relationship? Now, just as you did in the previous exercise, identify your negative communication practices and change them into positive ones. Correcting your negative communication habits and replacing them with positive ones helps you better understand, nurture, and support your mate.

The Effective Communication Gene

Many people consider good communication an innate skill or that there is a good communication gene which makes us magically effective. Nothing could be farther from the truth. Effective communication is a learned and practiced skill. Granted, children whose parents are good communicators tend to be as well, which makes it all more important for you and your mate to work at correcting your negative patterns. That way when your children are born they will have positive communication role models in their parents.

Five Traits of Effective Communicators

- *The ability to motivate others.* When you help your mate discover the talents she hides from herself and from the world, it moves her to action. This is accomplished with good communication skills. Being a good listener is part of being a good communicator. Therefore, when you listen well and praise well, you are capable of offering guidance and motivation.
- *The ability to encourage cooperation and build trust.* If your mate feels as if you are listening to his ideas and taking them seriously, it will strengthen his trust in you and his willingness to cooperate.
- *The ability to focus on the issue at hand.* Being able to discuss issues with your mate without straying off the path or bringing up unresolved hurts from the past is good for communication. When you focus on the issue at hand, you retain all the information necessary to resolve any conflict and you avoid any extraneous argument or discussion.
- *The ability to provide accurate and factual information.* Good communicators gather and share factual information with their mates. This ensures that both their discussions and their decisions are based on fact, not rumor.
- *The ability to prevent communication breakdowns.* Keeping the lines of communication open between you and your mate is critical to your relationship. When one mate does all the talking and the other all the listening, the couple suffers a communication breakdown. If there are problems or decisions to be made, both of you need to participate otherwise it is not a joint venture.

As in previous chapters, I advise you to review this chapter and find the communication skills where you feel the need for coaching and improvement. Share your goals with your mate, and create a self-coaching plan together.

Our Action Plan to Improve Communication

1. What is one area of communication we would like to improve?
2. How will improving our communication skills in this area affect our life together?
3. What steps can we take to achieve better communication in this area?
4. What do we hope to achieve by taking these steps?

Summary

In this chapter, you have learned that good communication skills are a learned behavior that requires practice and patience. You have also learned that with a bit of concentrated effort you can avoid communication pitfalls. It is important to have accurate expectations when discussing the issues and problems that arise in every relationship. This helps build trust, support, and security—three parts of a loving relationship that all parents hope to share with their children.

Wallet Card

- I am mindful about what and how I speak.
- I deal with inappropriate behavior, not analyze.
- I balance criticism with praise.
- I act on fact, not opinion.

CHAPTER EIGHT

The Third Secret

Solving Problems and Resolving Conflict

CHAPTER OBJECTIVES:

- Learn how to anticipate new-parent problems and solve them logically.
- Learn how appropriate conflict resolution equals success.
- Learn what your emotional reactions to conflict are.
- Learn alternative methods of handling conflict through personal life-coaching.

How you think about a problem is more important than the problem itself—so always think positively.

—Norman Vincent Peale

Have you got a problem? Do what you can where you are with what you've got.

—Theodore Roosevelt

A major secret to being successful new parents lies within your ability to solve problems and manage conflict. "Handling" the troubles and tribulations of everyday life in a productive manner will save you from distress. These bold statements are made because being a new parent is the one and only time in your life for which you cannot really prepare for the major transition. How to respond to conflict is determined by your emotional *reactions.*

In this chapter, you learn how effective conflict resolution can equal success. You will conduct an assessment of your reactions to conflict. By using the life-coaching tips in this chapter, you and your mate will discover the best ways of handling conflict and develop a plan for solving problems. As a result you will be able to foresee problems related to new parenting, develop a method of resolving them and more effectively manage future conflict.

Every relationship, when under pressures of planning, learning, and anticipating pregnancy and birth, must be able to face personal and family challenges that arise. Is it often a difficult time? Yes, and everyone gets through it. Wouldn't you like to be the couple who sails through with smiles on your faces and hearts filled with love, rather than frustration? Every relationship will encounter times when ideas differ, opinions clash or miscommunication results. However, it is possible to disagree without being disagreeable. Not all problems or conflicts need to result in having a negative effect. If you and your mate apply the effective methods that I present for you to achieve a resolution, you can both learn from the experience. You will also be able to maintain and build upon your positive attitudes about patiently and lovingly coaching yourselves through the process.

Exercise: Assess How You Handle Conflict

Choose the answers that best reflect your responses to the statements below:

1. When someone is hostile toward me, I tend to

A Respond with anger
B Use persuasion
C Take the abuse
D Walk away

2. When addressing others during a serious conflict, I have a tendency to

A Shout
B Listen a little
C Listen actively
D Apologize

3. When I am involved in an unpleasant confrontation, I

A Use sarcasm
B Joke occasionally
C Use humor related to me
D Use no humor

4. Following a serious conflict, I

A Settle things my way
B Negotiate an outcome
C Worry, but hide it
D Let it go

5. Others tell me that when I am faced with a serious problem, that I

A Fight for my way
B Show cooperation
C Am easygoing
D Avoid confrontation

6. When I am involved in a dispute, I generally

A Sway others
B Use logic
C Compromise
D Back down

Analyze Your Responses

Next, review your responses and determine which ones are more predominant for your style of reacting to problems or conflict. For example, do you often back down and avoid confrontation at all costs? Do you give in while compromising your own needs? Or, do you usually settle things in your own way, regardless of the other person's feelings or desires? If you have a tendency to react to conflict using these types of unproductive methods, then you may profitably consider altering your conflict-resolution style. More productive methods of solving problems use logic and resolve conflict through compromise, while actively listening and cooperating so that both of you can be satisfied with the outcome.

Anticipating New Parent Problems

The best plan for problem solving during pregnancy and when you bring your baby home is for both of you to anticipate the problems that will arise and develop your plan of solutions. Make your decisions now about how you will handle any conflict such as being overstressed with little sleep or needing to get away. Determine what information you will need. Work out your solutions prior to the appearance of problems. Develop a Plan A and then a Plan B of solutions so you can feel safe knowing how easily any problem could be addressed and taken care of.

As one of my younger clients, Liesel, a brand new mother, said, "I was so fascinated by my pregnancy, the bodily changes, and the baby's development. I was so in the moment that I never thought much about what happens when the baby arrives. Then suddenly the nine months were gone, and we were bringing Lisa home. Oh goodness, there were so many little things I needed to know."

Like Liesel, most new parents focus on the pregnancy and birth preparation. Yet, after the birth, couples wake up to the fact that birth is the first step in a journey of many years. Taking steps before delivery to prepare for parenting can help enormously. Your mental and emotional preparation is just as important as preparing the nursery. To anticipate any problems that you may encounter as a new parent, I have prepared a list of questions for your review below. These questions are not problems. They are questions for your learning. *Do I need more information about this topic? Have we considered this situation? Do we have the answers we need just in case there is a problem?* Make notes in your journal, and use them later to develop a plan to anticipate and resolve possible problems. Resolving possible problem areas might be as easy as finding a good book on breastfeeding or your desire to consult with a financial advisor to insure that you feel secure in the next stage of parenting.

Pregnancy and Birthing Questions:

- How will you handle morning sickness?
- What are your birthing options?

- Should you use the services of a midwife or doula?
- What support do you have for a night out now and then?
- What are your risks for gestational diabetes or any other genetic issues within your family medical histories?
- As a professional couple, how will you handle medical emergencies?
  - How will you handle time away from work?
  - Is someone at work on board to cover for you if you are away?
  - Do you have a friend to call as back-up if you have an emergency or need transportation?
  - Are there family members nearby whom you can call?
  - Have you considered hiring a parent coach?

Financial issues

- Do you have life insurance for yourself and your child in the event of your death or your child's death?
- Will you set up a college fund for your child now, and plan for her future?

An Emergency Fund

You may need extra cash flow on hand after the baby's birth because in the first month, you will be determining which swings, cribs, or bassinets and such that you want to purchase for your child. Consider what happened to Jennifer. She delivered a 9-pound baby who did not fit in the bassinet that all of the grandchildren in the immediate family had used. Yet, he was too tiny for the big crib. Jennifer and her husband tried two co-sleeper beds, which pushed them out of their queen-sized bed. Finally, rather than worry about various baby beds, they bought themselves a king-size bed where their son could nurse and sleep with them. Also their friends had showered them with disposable diapers for their newborn, but he was allergic to the plastic. They had to find a diaper service immediately to deliver cloth diapers. Fortunately they had set aside extra dollars to use for such purposes. Learn from their example.

Legal Issues:

- Who will serve as your child's guardian if one or both of you are incapacitated or die?
- Who do you want to rear your children in your absence? Do you have legal power of attorney prepared and signed now?
- Have you left a will with assets allocated for your child's support?
- Do you have a living will for appropriate medical treatment in the event that you are incapacitated?

In the First Two Months When Baby Comes Home:

- Do you need to arrange for postpartum assistance?
  - A relative?
  - A neighbor?
  - A doula or parent coach?
  - Someone in your church community?
- Will you need personal emotional support, as a father, or as a mother?
  - Parent support group?
  - Internet support group?
  - Parent Coaching support?
  - Counselor or pastor?
  - Start your own support group?
- What kind of household supplies might you need?
  - One month's worth of meals?
  - Feminine napkins?
  - Medical supplies for baby?
  - Supplies for dehydration for the mom after receiving any medications?
  - Diaper supply service or a stock of diapers?

  - Pain management for Mom for cramping, episiotomy, or C-section recovery?
- Will you be breastfeeding or bottle-feeding?
  - What are the proper "latch–on" procedures for a newborn?
  - What kind of family support will you need?
  - What kind of breast pump serves you? Learn about pumping and storing milk.
  - Learn the common early breastfeeding problems.
  - If you are a working mom, what breastfeeding issues will you encounter at work?
  - Learn about introducing a bottle.

Problem Solving

Anyone can solve a problem, and very few people know how to do it. Some people have difficulty paying attention to the detail of defining what the real problem is. Others cannot focus on the issue at hand. Because attention and focus are the two foundational steps to solving a problem, it is difficult if not impossible to determine a solution until there is a plan. Applying a problem-solving solution in the early stages of being a new parent will save you so many headaches, distress and problems. Here's how to develop a plan of possible solutions for the problems that you anticipate.

State the Problem or Ask the Question Clearly

As a new parent you will experience some tough, but loving times: Lack of sleep, extreme fatigue, dehydration, and over-stressed nerves that cause you to not think clearly and instead to react. We will address the stress management aspect in Chapter 9, but for now, let's follow Charles Kettering's advice. Kettering, a prolific and ingenious inventor, said that a "problem clearly stated is a problem half-solved."

Exercise

So review the list of questions above. Brainstorm together and write down any questions you need answered or which reveal anticipated problems. Clearly state the problems you anticipate under each major area. For example,

- What are my options if the baby does not latch-on during breastfeeding?
- What are my food choices for the first four weeks of meals?
- As a new mom, who can I talk to about the issues I will face?

Don't Fall Back into Emotional Reaction

What is problem solving really? In part, it is anticipating obstacles on the path to your goals. In part, it is deciphering your internal emotional signals along the way or being aware of environmental signals. Think about the simple everyday problems like finding lost keys or what to do when your car won't start. We encounter these and walk through a simple pattern to complete our goal. For lost keys, you will use a familiar problem-solving approach of looking in the familiar places, probably several times. If you do not find the keys, you won't give up. Instead, you will turn inward and let your intuition remember your path you took where you think you lost them. Ah yes, there are the keys in the laundry room when you carried in a load of detergent and threw everything on top the washer for the moment!

Remember in the previous chapter on self-esteem, you read that people become overwhelmed when they are in unfamiliar territory and find they can't think clearly enough to even state the problem. New parenting constitutes unfamiliar territory. Find some humor in Chris and Adrian's story.

Adrian's mom, Esther, showed up several days before Adrian was scheduled for induced labor. Esther realized that Adrian was already in labor and went immediately to the hospital with the family. Chris and Adrian stayed in the hospital for two full days and nights, and Esther returned to the family's small townhouse to start cleaning up and cooking for the family. Esther was used to living in the Northeast where summers are cool and her daughter and son-in-law lived in the Southwest. Adrian flipped on the air conditioner to 65 degrees. The house cooled down, and Esther was happy as she could be in preparing the way for her new granddaughter to come home.

When Chris and Adrian walked into their house, the first thing they noticed was water dripping from the ceiling onto their dining room table. At first the two numbed-out parents, having been without sleep for 48 hours, stared at the drips. But there was no laundry room or bathroom above that area, and there was no hole or crack in the ceiling. There seemed to be no cause, and thus no solution; Adrian lost it.

She screamed at her husband to do something. So he went upstairs as expected to check out the hallway, in which he knew he would find nothing. Esther had both new parents sit down, and ask the questions to which they needed answers. The obvious solution was to call the maintenance crew for the town homes. That led to the next step of calling the HVAC technician, who informed them that they couldn't turn their fifteen year-old air conditioner on 65 degrees without the machine sweating off the condensation and leaking into their dining room. The problem was solved. Keep the thermostat on 72!

Coach Yourself to Solve the Problem

When circumstances change, old procedures no longer work. When Adrian saw the dripping, she screamed, overwrought in her exhaustion and fatigue. Chris, to keep her happy, checked the hallway to make sure there were no leaks. Unless you coach yourself in the following skills, you will likewise respond to problems or conflicts from an emotional space and not from one of common sense or logic.

Adaptation To adapt is to pursue valued goals even when circumstances—and perhaps the goals themselves—are in flux.

Conserve Your Energy Spend only 5% of your energy on talking about the problem, and 95% of your energy on solving the problem.

Define the Problem Clearly understand and identify the problem. Describe and label the problem in precise and concrete terms.

Rephrase the Problem or Potential Problem as a Question For example, "Linda can't drive me to work" identifies a potential problem. However, it may or may not be the problem depending on other factors. The definition above describes the cause of a potential problem. Rephrasing the problem to "How will I get to work?" puts the focus of the problem-solving on arriving to work rather than on the fact that Linda got sick that day.

Develop Alternative Solutions This is better known as brainstorming, a technique using stream-of-consciousness listing of solutions in which no idea is a bad one. Each idea could be a possible solution. Seek to predict your ability to accomplish the actions of each solution and predict the consequences. In Adrian and Chris' problem with water drops in the dining room, they had to brainstorm whom to call. A plumber was their first idea. But in brainstorming together, the no-cost option was to get an opinion from the maintenance man for the units. Not only did it save the time and cost of arranging a plumber's visit, the solution was simple when the right expert showed up.

Make the Best Decision Make a decision and then carry it out. Most people think that their problem is solved once they have made their crucial decision. However, there is one more step before going into action.

Evaluate the Outcome This is where a lot of learning takes place. What is the anticipated outcome? If it is agreed upon as suitable by both of you, then take action. If the outcome was successful, then those involved learn that the solution was a good one and will use it again if the problem resurfaces.

Every problem is an opportunity for growth, learning, and keeping an open mind.

Incorporating Problem-Solving Skills into Your Lives

As new parents, read and practice these skills for parenting success as well as for your personal clarity and competence. By applying a little thoughtfulness in tense times, these coaching skills can become the habits you need to prevent conflicts and solve problems. The essential skills to possess are to:

1. Use effective communication.
2. Avoid overreacting.
3. Eliminate confusion.
4. Identify and avoid disruptive behavior.
5. Use creativity and keep an open mind.

The following are explanations of the above problem-solving skills to help you plan your best possible solutions with effective communication and logic.

Problem-Solving Skill 1: Use effective communication.

Miscommunication is usually the underlying fault of confrontation. Usually one person assumes the other knew exactly what a statement meant. Always ask for clarity if necessary, "Do you understand? Do you have any questions?" Communicate your needs and your solutions clearly, and don't expect your mate to read your mind. Everyone needs to learn a few basic rules of communication and practice using them until it becomes natural as you learned in the previous chapter.

Problem-Solving Skill 2: Avoid overreacting.

Conflict can cause your emotions to rise high, and overreaction is an emotion that is usually not effective. It is much better to take a deep breath, catch yourself before overreacting, and redirect your focus. Can you find a positive comment to make, a question of clarity to ask, or a suggestion that would discharge the intensity of the moment?

If you react to conflict by not speaking up, this is an equally ineffective solution. When you hold emotions inside and do not express what you are feeling, the emotions can take over and overwhelm your rational thinking. Do not let emotions build up. Discharge them by discussing your feelings when you are calm. When possible, wait twenty-four hours before you react to a highly emotional issue. In the interim write down your thoughts and feelings so that you can discuss them once you've calmed down.

Problem-Solving Skill 3: Eliminate confusion.

To eliminate confusion during a heated moment, return to a calming pattern of deep breathing and let any charged emotions pass. To clarify the communication, ask questions: *Can you explain that one more time? Is this your point? Can you describe the problem from your viewpoint? Can you tell me your point in a few sentences? Do you need to calm down first? Would you like a break now and we can return to our discussion later?* This immediately shifts the focus of the confrontation to the person and away from the actual problem. When in a conflict, diffuse anger by insisting that everyone concentrate on the initial problem and put aside any extraneous issues. This is a worthwhile if sometimes difficult task.

Problem-Solving Skill 4: Identify and avoid disruptive behavior.

When a person is engaging is disruptive behavior, it is important for you to understand that he has an underlying reason for the behavior and is not conveying that clearly and logically. Find out why. That is the big question to answer before any resolution can be discussed. Put yourself in the place of the person you consider difficult and ask yourself, *Why is she acting like this? What is he getting out of it?*

Studies have shown that when a person is rewarded for any type of behavior, that reward acts as reinforcement to continue along the same path. Perhaps, the acting-out person receives a payoff of attention or an emotional release. Maybe the acting-out person uses this behavior unconsciously for manipulation. So what is the reward that this person receives from acting in such a manner? Is this a habit or a one-time response triggered by some external event?

Remember, you cannot change other people's behavior, but you can change the way you react to their behavior.

Problem-Solving Skill 5: Use creativity and keep an open mind.

An open mind during confrontation or problem solving still welcomes another person's ideas and solutions despite any conflict. Having an open mind, to most people, means to listen or to hear with attention. But an open mind is more than polite listening. Having an open mind implies not judging the situation, conflict, or ideas. In cases of discussion, where answers and solution are being provided, being open-minded means welcoming those ideas.

Sometimes it takes the combined efforts of more than one person to get ideas flowing. Not all suggestions will be good, but they can lead to ideas and thoughts that will help determine the best outcome. The ideal situation is one in which, after a problem is recognized, all parties involved meet to consider alternative methods of approach and compromise. Learn how to come up with creative solutions to problems. Avoid being stuck in a never-ending argument. Know how and when to compromise using creative alternatives.

Develop a New Parent Plan to Solve Problems and Resolve Conflict

It is also important to determine exactly what outcome you are after. You know through your self-coaching the value of goals and action steps to your achieving success. The first step is to determine and list your personal guidelines in each of your journals.

Our Family's Guidelines

Examples: Each person will share his feelings and needs.
Each person's ideas are welcome.
Each person will contribute ideas alternatively without critical comment.

You and your mate are now ready to be effective in your role as problem solvers. One last caution: Be sure to invoke the Rule of the Five P's: Proper Preparation Prevents Poor Performance.

Prior to engaging a problem and attempting a solution, define it clearly. Do not assume that all information you receive is accurate and valid. Check your sources and determine that they are reliable and that you have honest, unbiased information. Next, develop a plan that you can follow when a conflict arises within your partnership and family. Here is a model plan for your use. Read it through, and then modify it for your use:

Model Plan for Solving Problems and Resolving Conflict

1. State the issue in writing.
2. Write down each person's suggested solutions.
3. Agree on a resolution to the problems and write it down.
4. Write down ways to carry out the solutions
5. Take the action steps outlined in your plan.
6. Follow up on your hard work and evaluate the results of your actions.

Summary

In this chapter, you learned that how you cope with the fluctuations of life is in large part determined by your reactions to problems or conflicts. You learned how proper conflict resolution can lead you to success. You and your mate have assessed your reactions to conflict. As a result you can anticipate the problems that new parents face and how to ask the right questions to get the answers you need. You also discovered methods of handling conflict and resolving problems. Finally, you and your family developed a conflict-resolution plan.

Wallet Card

- Ask the proper questions and educate myself in anticipation of our pregnancy.
- Effective conflict resolution can lead to success.
- Remember the Rule of the Five P's: Proper Preparation Prevents Poor Performance.
- Creatively search with my mate for new solutions to old problems.

CHAPTER NINE

The Fourth Secret

Managing Stress

CHAPTER OBJECTIVES:

- Identify your stressors and your reactions to stress.
- Learn that your response to stress is subject to your control.
- Learn to embrace stress as a challenge to growth and maturity.
- Identify gender differences in stress responses.
- Understand the role that stress plays in pregnancy.

Stress is not what happens to us. It's our response *to* what happens.
And *response* is something we can choose.

—Maureen Killoran

"When you find yourself stressed, ask yourself one question:
Will this matter 5 years from now? If yes, then do something about
the situation. If no, then let it go."

—Catherine Pulsifer

It's All In How You See It!

Stress is common to everyone, and the human body and mind are designed to respond to stress effectively. The body is designed to move through life in a certain rhythm that is comfortable for you. When the rhythm speeds up and events happen faster than you can reasonably respond to them or cope with them, then distress occurs. The body stops and needs rest and balance.

In this chapter, you will learn how to define stress and coping responses for yourself and your mate. You'll understand how to assess the stressors in your life and how to view stress as your friend challenging you to excel. In addition, you will learn ways to support each other through the stress that comes to all new parents.

Definitions

The two words to define clearly are **stress** and **management**. A simple definition of stress is when you feel stretched beyond your ability to successfully engage a condition, situation, or person. Your ability to manage under the imposed pressure is described as the skill of coping. Stress management or coping then is being able to both survive and also deal with the physical and the mental aspects of your stress reactions. Let's discuss each one in more depth.

Stress: What becomes stress for you depends upon your perceptions and reactions to the stressor. A perception is how you view or see things and includes value judgments like good and bad. A reaction is an emotional response, often from past memories of similar experiences, that overrides reason, like jumping after a loud noise or pulling away from a hot flame. Whether or not something is stressful depends on your personal point of view. For example, a high achiever who thrives on accomplishment may love to travel three weeks out of every month. The further he travels and the more people he meets fills him with joy. He thrives on high stimulation and contact with a lot of people. On the other hand, a homebody who enjoys a slower pace of activity would be stressed out by the high achiever's busy schedule. The homebody relaxes in the quiet atmosphere and enjoys a few, close friends. The high achiever might become equally stressed by the *lack* of stimulus and boredom in the homebody's environment.

Stress is your personal reaction to any stimulus that requires you to adjust or respond outside of your normal limits.

The secret of understanding stress and its management lies within the phrase "your reaction" and "beyond normal limits." Because stress comes from how you personally respond to stressful events, know then that you have the power to control stress through your self-coaching program.

Stressor + your perception of stressor = your response to stress

Management: To manage stress effectively includes your ability to

- Identify your stressors.
- Recognize your physical and psychological reactions to stress.
- Determine if the stress is stretching or enhancing you in a positive way, or
- Determine if stress persists to an excessive degree.

Where stress enhances your physical and mental functions, consider it good stress. However, prolonged stress or intense bouts of stress eventually leads to a need for resolution and can result in withdrawing, confronting, or escaping types of behavior.

Identification of Stressors

A stressor is an event, which can be internal or external, that can trigger your anxiety. An example of an internal event is demonstrated in Miriam's story. At thirty years of age, Miriam entered parenthood for the first time. Her estrogen levels dropped below normal after the baby was born. The results were mood swings, irritability, anxiety, hot flashes, sleepless nights and bouts of negative thinking. Her physician gave her a prescription to help with these mood swings, and Miriam sat down to read the booklet explaining the side effects of the medication. The list of estrogen related difficulties such as breast cancer, cervical cancer, uterine cancer and more was so horrifying to Miriam that she became physically sick to her stomach and went to bed. Miriam scared herself by reading the list and imagining all of the symptoms until she felt ill, from her imagined, overblown representation of the facts. This contributed to her catastrophic thinking, leading to increased stress.

An example of an externally triggered event is demonstrated in Rick's story. Rick and Crystal were married straight out of high school because they were deeply in love with each other. Rick held a steady job for several years, but desired more education and stability for his new family after Crystal announced that she was pregnant. They agreed that Rick would enter the army. Rick was deployed to the Middle East two months before his son was born. Rick described his response to the news of his son's birth: "I thought my response was strange because I felt like I had no control over my emotions. When Crystal sent a video of Luke's birth, I was thrilled and cried at sight of my little boy. At the same time I was angry at being where I am, and I wanted to pound my fist against a wall. I didn't know I could be excited, happy, and angry all in the same emotional wave. I was pumping so much adrenaline that I couldn't sleep for a week."

External stressors represent natural life events as well as incidents that anyone could face every day or within their lifetime. Every day you may cope with

- Deadlines
- Traffic
- Money problems
- Arguments or confrontations
- Organizing and managing a household or a business

In your lifetime you will certainly face and have to deal with

- Death
- Illnesses
- Accidents
- Relocation
- Marriage
- Pregnancy
- Job change

Other issues that rate high as stressors can include family concerns like divorce, adoption or being a foster parent, bringing home a new baby, legal problems, coping with an aging parent, facing retirement, addictions, and prolonged or terminal illness.

Exercise: Identifying Stressors

As you review this list above, make a summary in your journal about the major life events that have occurred for you within the last year. The more events that have occurred for you, the higher your stressors will be. Because of the human body's magnificent ability to cope and be resilient, people may not be aware of the slow impact of stress as it accumulates over time. Then it will be important for you to compare the list of stressors with your perception of stress. Determine these two factors:

1. How many major life events you have been through, and
2. How you have responded to those events. Then, you can plan better for all the preparations and timing for being new parents. When you can control the timing of events, then you can control some of the stressors and your responses.

For example, William and Joyce had been trying to get pregnant for over a year. During this time, they shared much delight in planning to move from a two-bedroom condo to a single-family home with a yard. They spoke of having a dog along with a child since Joyce would be at home full time for at least one year, and they enjoyed the idea that their son or daughter would grow up with a pet as each of them had. They took Sundays to look at new homes and secretly redecorate them in their minds.

Then the bottom dropped out of the real estate market. Their real estate advisor suggested that they take their condo off the market for a while. Their dreams of their new family, pet, and home suddenly vanished. Meantime they found out that they were pregnant and discussed how they would adapt in their small condo. They set their goal for a new home within two years, and determined to wait on a pet.

William and Joyce took their dreams in stride and did not overtax themselves. The delivery of their healthy child was their most important goal, and they adjusted their dreams and timelines accordingly in a healthy way: through discussion, an assessment of finances, and a review of their goals and re-prioritizing their desires for the next two years.

Recognition of Stress Facts and Responses

Your response to stress is an adaptation to your environment. When change happens, you stretch to accommodate the transformation that is required. You may know that in the field of life coaching, stress is synonymous with personal growth. Throughout this book, the life coaching tips and subsequent goals you have set for yourself stretch you to the next level for learning, growing emotionally and gaining new insight. Let's look at the logic of how we view stress.

Fact: Life is about change and transitions.

Fact: Stress is about how we cope or respond to change and transitions.

Fact: Modern man responds to stressors in the same autonomic reaction patterns as the ancestral cave men and women: slower digestion, faster breathing, pumping heart and increased perspiration, augmented blood clotting chemicals and increased sugars for fuel. You also respond to stress in this pattern. Whether you see it as a helpful or a distressing response depends upon your perception. Read on!

Fact: So people are prepared to fight, to flee, and sometimes, just freeze. However people seldom fight or flee nowadays. Rather most individuals try to get through the day and contain their nervous energy. Others, remaining mostly fatigued, try to pump their energy up with caffeine and sugar.

Fact: Smaller stressors and brief stress responses add up to hundreds per day. What are the results?

- Studies suggest that the inability to adapt to stress is associated with the onset of depression or anxiety. In one study, two-thirds of subjects who experienced a stressful situation had nearly six times the risk of developing depression within that month.[1]
- Mental stress as well as physical exertion can trigger angina.
- There is a high correlation between stress and hypertension.

Fact: Knowing that different types of change will affect all of us, the choice about cultivating positive and peaceful stress responses becomes not only your choice, but your responsibility, especially with a new family in your plans.

View Stress in a Positive Light

All stress is not harmful. When seen in a positive or helpful way, stress can spur us to creativity and insight as well as good planning. Learn self-coaching skills to manage your stress responses. Stress is a fact of life and to attempt to make it go away or change the externals of your life is ineffective. What is most effective or purposeful is learning to alter your inner rhythm by employing relaxation skills and adapting internally to a busy outer world.

There are winners in the game of life who have cultivated relaxation responses. These winners still face what you face and certainly feel anxiety. What makes them different is they do not focus on their fears and anxieties. Rather, they seek the challenge or the opportunity for growth. Like the winner, you can focus on your strengths, the survival skills that got you where you are, and learn how to maximize them when confronting change, transition or trauma.

Consider an athlete in training. Her coach will develop stress exercises to stretch muscles to the next movement or position of strength. Then repetitions are necessary for maximizing a good, healthy habit. For an athlete, the stressors may be the vehicle by which to achieve dreams. Athletes cannot go to the next level by freezing, fleeing, or fighting; yet a sportsman can use the fighting spirit and the adrenaline for his achievement. Don't fear or worry about stress. See stress as a fact of life and make stress your friend by building an athlete's repertoire of coping behaviors.

Author James E. Loehr said, "Getting control of our personal chemistry, getting control of our emotions, getting control of our stress is all one and the same . . . Perception dictates chemistry. Change your perception and change your chemistry."[2]

Gender Differences in Stress Responses

The prototypical responses to stress, mentioned above, as the flight or fight reactions have dominated the stress research for decades. Most of this research was conducted on men, who were considered to be more stable test subjects than women. Women's endocrine responses and mood fluctuations were more difficult variables to control in research situations. It wasn't until twelve years ago that the National Institute of Health finally recognized women's medicine as a separate area of research and documentation. The results speak loudly to the differences in how men and women respond to stress. This point is vitally important for you as new parents to understand and plan around in your new family. You want be each other's support and friend in the stressors of pregnancy and starting a new family.

- Women complain more about minor stress symptoms such as headaches or shoulder tension, whereas men tend to be quieter regarding symptoms and have a greater stress response at one time.
- Women suffer fewer long-term related problems such as cardiovascular disease. This could be indicative of men keeping their symptoms to themselves or being unaware of the longer-term effects of chronic stress.
- Researchers once thought that women release more stress hormones like cortisol and epinephrine, thus they are moodier. However there is no consistent difference in the production of these hormones in men and women.
- Instead, the hormone oxytocin plays a role. In women, oxytocin counters the harsh impact of the stress hormones and promotes nurturing and relaxing emotions. Men also produce oxytocin, but in smaller amounts, causing them to bottle stress up or desire to escape from it.
- Social orientation indicates that women seek social support, while men are more likely to turn to a drink or drugs for coping.
- The "nice-girl" orientation of the submissive woman tends to exaggerate health symptoms when emotions are kept inside or unexpressed.
- The "hold-it-in" syndrome for men finds that men have difficulty admitting insecurities and dealing with conflict.
- The greatest stressor for men is performance failure; the greatest stressor for women is relationship loss as well as dependency.

The researchers would agree that women probably manage stress better than men due to the cascade of hormones that enable women to nurture and seek support from other women. Another way to say that is that women seek health-supporting stress management and, in general, men may reach for stress reduction through approaches that do not support long-term health.

How Pregnancy Is a Stressful Time and What You Can Do About It!

In the book *Stress Management for Dummies,* author Allen Elkin, Ph.D., listed the birth of a child as one of the top ten stressors, at least in Western culture. Birth and being a new parent are stressful, and also joyful, exhausting, exhilarating, worrisome, awesome, and a whole bundle of mixed emotions wrapped up in the moment of watching your child enter the world.

We spoke in the previous chapter of the worries that you may face of not being in control of this aspect of your life. You learned how to plan ahead for probable problems and developed a plan for solving any issue you might encounter. Stress is one of those issues, and you can plan ahead by welcoming the stress that accompanies your new child and allow the resulting challenges to empower your growth. You have the responsibility to develop health-supportive responses to the stress-filled times. Here are six reasons why:

1. Each of you will have separate fears that accompany not being in total control of this part of your life. As a woman, you may want to talk about your image of being a mother and how you will deal with the pain of childbirth. As a man, you may choose to hold fears of financial responsibility and readiness inside. Yet, both of you will need to find ways to support each other through conversation. Put the fears on the table. List them on paper. As they change each day, cross the old out and list and discuss the new ones that arise. Keep the fears and concerns flowing throughout your conversations. Facing fears dissolves fears, and then you are done with it until next time. Make it a rule to hold no fears inside where they can fester into stress. As mates, find ways of conversing or communing that suit your styles and schedules.

2. Each of you will have concerns about your gender roles. List your concerns about being a new father or a new mother. If you were a professional taking leave to be a new parent, list any questions you have about your changing roles including questions about your duties, issues about time, or any expectations you perceive might be pushed onto you by your mate. List your solutions to perceived problems after your discussion. Here are some examples:

Concerns: Can I respond to my wife and run the errands and manage the household?

Solution: Make a list of the weekly errands and ask a friend or parent to make a weekly run for supplies or groceries.

Solution: List all anticipated problems and delegate the responsibility to others. Hire a professional assistant or mother's helper for one month.

3. Each of you will have heightened sensitivity to deal with. Women, you may feel heightened sensitivity to sound, noise, pressure, physical sensations and other environmental stimuli. Men, you will feel your wife's heightened sensitivity and need to develop your sympathy and compassion to assist where you can. Can you go to each doctor's appointment, guide important decision-making as a couple, write down the questions to which you need answers, and anticipate problems she might not see? Can you be a calm and supportive birth mate, or would a female be better for your wife when she is in labor?

For instance, one couple made their first rule of new parenting as "Don't take me personally." The small slights, irritations and tension with each other can be dismissed with a deep breath, a hug, and a plan to relax. Does each of you need a foot massage, a hot bath or just quiet time alone?

4. You might desire a new parent coach or mentor who can assist you with the large and small questions and anticipate the stressors for you. An up and coming trend is for new parents to have a midwife, doula, or parent coach to educate them on the new parent journey. Do you remember the young woman from a previous chapter who indicated that she have put so much education into being pregnant that she was shocked she knew nothing about the baby's arrival? A mentor can guide you to find the effective answers, assist in the birth-plan as well as the coming-home-plan, and ease your stress.

5. New parents need to get healthier, faster. The first step that new parents take when they discover that they are pregnant is to shop—for a home, for the nursery, for toys or a stuffed animal. Resist the urge. If you do indulge it, then promise yourself after the shopping fun, to sit down together and make a list of how you can make your lifestyles healthier. Do you eat healthy selections of hormone and antibiotic-free meats, pesticide-free vegetables and fruits, and whole grains? Does your exercise program include a walk of at least twenty minutes every day? Will you incorporate relaxation regimens from the next chapter into your week? Can you cook and exercise together?

6. New Parents must plan relaxation regimens or resilience building into their pregnancy plan. Research shows that overly-stressed pregnant women release cortisol, and the stress hormone cross the placenta. Babies with higher levels of stress chemicals tend to be quicker to cry. Another study found that unhappy relationships during pregnancy produced children who were five times more fearful and jumpy than the children of good relationships. The next chapter provides a variety of activities to empower your strength, embrace stress and enjoy this miraculous time as new parents.

Summary

In this chapter, you learned that stress is your response to an internal or external event that you perceive as stretching you beyond your coping abilities. When stressors cause acute or chronic problems, then you deal with distress. Your perception of stress is the ultimate factor in whether you just survive or whether you can learn to thrive. Men and women deal with stress differently, and this affects your roles as mates and new parents. Because stress affects the baby's behavior and emotional calm, I highly suggest you read on to develop a resilience plan for your pregnancy.

Wallet Card

- I view stress as a challenge to help me learn.
- I am sensitive to my mate's needs.
- I will create a healthier lifestyle to support my new role as a parent.
- I will develop a resilience plan with my mate.

PART THREE

REACHING YOUR NEW PARENTING SUCCESS POTENTIAL

CHAPTER TEN

The Fifth Secret

Building a Resilience Reserve

CHAPTER OBJECTIVES

- Understand the importance and impact of resilience.
- Learn how resilience can help ease you into being new parents.
- Develop and build a program for a resilience reserve.
- Plan lifestyle changes that support your resilience.

The bamboo that bends is stronger than the oak that resists.

—Japanese Proverb

Get revenge by living well instead of squandering your energy by blaming and fault-finding.

—Steve Wolin and Sybil Wolin

In the previous chapter, which discussed stress management, you learned that your point of view or perception is the over-riding factor in dealing with stressors and adversity. You now know that you are able to control your reactions and, instead, substitute responses whenever stressful situations arise. In this chapter, I will walk you through easy-to-learn stress management tools which you can use to train yourself in positive responses to stress.

In your coaching strategies, you built into your planning the positive belief that stressors are your friendly reminders to stretch, grow and learn. Taking this psychological approach allows you to feel emotions deeply, move through them as necessary, and still be aware and focused with your responses to daily confrontation or stress.

The ability to bounce back from setback, to keep moving forward and learning from life is called resilience. Resilience is a skill you can develop which involves focusing on inner resources and developing preventive strategies so that you have time for relaxation and renewal. You will learn how to regulate emotions associated with stress to manage tension and facilitate relaxation.

A planned response to stress would include both changing the demand of the stressor in the environment and also taking steps to expand your internal capacity to deal with issues. To respond to external stressors, you examine your options and evaluate your resources before responding. For example if your stress tends to make you feel nervous or anxious, perhaps you would significantly reduce your intake of caffeine to help you remain calm. You could also include calming foods in your diet. Alternatively you could alter your sleeping pattern to accommodate a greater need for rest or spend more time stretching and walking to relieve tension.

To deal with internal stressors, you can expand or build up your internal capacity to handle stressors through a variety of self-coaching resources found in this chapter. The primary foundation, as you read in the previous chapter, is to focus on the positive challenge inherent in your response, and learn to extend and expand your coping skills. For example, a person who has a commute to work each day could be exposing herself to a high-stress time; even current studies indicate that commuting each day can cause a driver to have a panic attack. All you can control is the environment within your car as well as your internal feelings. People using self-coaching principles often listen to music or turn their attention to talk shows. Some persons use stretching exercises to relieve tension if their commute requires sitting for more than 30 minutes. Others do not drink their morning coffee while driving if they tend to express anger or irritability. The key is to moderate your internal or external environment so that you can be focused and positive. It is the only way to be to maintain resilience.

Authors and psychologists Reivich and Shatte describe resilience as a habit of mind. Their book, *The Resilience Factor,* describes resilience as the end result and benefit of your learning curve in dealing with stressors. Your resilience enables you to adjust to shock, disturbance, insult, or distress. Being resilient implies that you have flexibility, like the bamboo that bends.

Assess Your Resilience

Exercise

Please respond to each question below with a Yes or No. Think back over the last six months about stressful changes that have occurred. Let's call such events SC (stressful changes). As you review your responses to SC, please answer the following questions in your journal.

1.	My immediate response to SC is to observe or assess.	Y	N
2.	Generally I am happy with how I respond to SC.	Y	N
3.	My feelings about SC can be pretty positive.	Y	N
4.	My thoughts stay fairly logical with SC.	Y	N
5.	I guard against negative thinking around SC.	Y	N
6.	I can remain calm in the face of SC.	Y	N
7.	Others tend to rely upon my common sense approach.	Y	N
8.	I learn something most of the time from SC.	Y	N
9.	I have a positive influence on others during SC times.	Y	N
10.	I am not overly wrought or fatigued throughout SC.	Y	N

Review

Give yourself 10 points for each YES answer and for each NO response. The higher your YES scores, the more resilient you are. If your NO responses totaled 30 or more, then in your journal, add goals which reflect the areas in which you would like to expand your resilience.

For example, if you had a score of thirty, pretend that these three general statements were your challenges for growth:

- I can remain calm in the face of SC.
- I guard against negative thinking around SC.
- I am not overly wrought or fatigued throughout SC.

The chances are that the person with these patterns may have an intense emotional response to stress and would not remain healthy under chronic stress since both patterns weaken the immune system's ability to defend against stress hormones. After experiencing highly charged emotions, the person would tend to be fatigued because the pumping adrenalin to support the stress has stopped, and the body requires a period of rest and recovery. The positively focused goals for the self-coaching plan could be this: *"When faced with SC, I breathe deeply into my abdomen and repeat the positive affirmation 'I am safe, and I can handle this.' Then I will respond calmly."* Obviously this will take practice, and who does practice this will have phenomenal control over their ability to respond to life. This chapter is full of other resilience-building strategies you could use with this goal. I advise you to build into your self-coaching plan several approaches that work for you. Deep breathing may work best one week, but closing your eyes and taking a brief vacation may be more relaxing for you in the evening.

Resilience Coaching Tips

1. Observe and Assess Most individuals who follow a self-coaching program have learned that there is a difference between anxious reactions to stressors and a planned response. Recently, I was on vacation, and while walking along a beach crowded with people, I watched an older man collapse in front of me. The people surrounding the man had varied reactions. The woman who I believe was his wife stared in a frozen, momentary panic before yelling for help. Another middle-aged woman standing nearby started crying loudly, causing alarm in several children. One thirty-something young woman stepped forward to administer CPR. Then she directed several people from those around her to varied tasks like calling 911 or finding a warm blanket. This example demonstrates that the woman who administered CPR observed the situation, assessed what was needed, and took action after the initial shock of watching a person collapse. She was the most resilient in her ability to respond clearly and quickly.

2. Logical Feelings The term "logical feelings" might seem paradoxical. However, when you respond to distress or intense change with true feelings of genuine hurt or pain, this is very logical. Release of pent-up feelings is a natural way to express yourself. Talking through charged feelings is also helpful in gaining perspective and moving to the view of assessing your available resources to be used for solutions.

3. Positive Perspective The ability to see positive outcomes of changes that occur leaves the door open for transformation and learning. To concentrate on the negative aspects instead causes depression and fatigue because of the effect negative thoughts have on the body's biochemistry. Putting your brain to work and anticipating a silver lining provides hope for a better outcome and supports your most response-able chemical state.

4. Holding Tension During times of distress such as dealing with prolonged illness of a loved one, facing surgery or recovering from a divorce, do you feel like you hold onto the tension? Do you imagine yourself to be like a stretched rubber band? Holding tension is a necessary survival skill we all need to develop, and it is important to remember that the body and mind can stretch effectively. They can only do this, however, with rest periods in between. Be sure to take recovery time. You need it because your system works best and grows stronger with alternating periods of stress—that wears you down—and recovery—that allows your system to regain strength or rebuild.

5. Remaining Calm It often appears as though the people who remain calmest during stressful times have the ability to influence others to remain calm. They remain unruffled, assess their situation, listen, and offer empathy. They help others to find their own solutions. As your own self-coach, calmness during the time of new parenting is an invaluable resource, especially when you can share it with your mate. Cultivate it now; build it into your life.

Stress Buffers Strengthen Your Resilience

Stress researchers have found certain character traits or qualities that can serve you well in gaining resilience. These qualities can be learned or cultivated with practice. The stress buffers include:

- **Social Support:** your network of friends, family, or community who can offer compassion in time of need.
- **Physical Fitness:** being in top shape, offers a strong resilience factor. The better your health and vitality, the better you withstand stress. Exercise in today's world in not a luxury; it is a necessity.
- **Consistency:** the ability to be reliable in your behavior. When you are functional and predictable (no, not to the point of boring!), your mate can count on you and trust you implicitly in this unfamiliar territory of pregnancy and new parenting. Each of you should be able to rely on each other and feel secure during this new parenting time.
- **A Sense of Humor:** While not all stressful situations leave room for humor, to find a sense of irony, to be able to joke or even to laugh until tears release the tensions are all helpful stress buffers.
- **Optimism:** Those with optimism are simply people who have hope and can offer hope to others.

Researchers call people who have several of these traits "hardy," because they seem to manage distress effectively. They are resilient people who do not take life so personally or as an affront. Even if they suffer emotionally from events, they know they will be all right in the long run. After all, life happens!

These qualities of resilience can help you determine which lifestyle choices move you smoothly along. However, who you are on the inside holds far more importance in your ability to be resilient. The following qualities of the heart are explained more thoroughly in later chapters. For now, understand that when you bring these qualities to your relationship and to your parenting, you connect with a tremendous inner capacity for love and happiness. These qualities of resilience will support you through your new parenting roles like a wave lifting you up and gently delivering you safely to shore. Surf's up!

- **Caring** is being considerate and thoughtful of other's needs. Pregnancy and being new parents truly requires that you have the utmost respect for each other's feelings and needs.
- **Commitment** is being responsible to another in your promises and obligations. As a new parent, you are committed to being educated and involved in this process. For example, a commitment to review your goals, plan weekly and assist your mate keep your self-coaching skills in the forefront of your busy lives.
- **Integrity** is remaining true to your values and is important for each of you as individuals in a relationship. For example, when tired and snapping at another, it is better to remember your value of respecting your mate first than to apologize later for hurtful words or actions that could have been prevented
- **Challenge** is enjoying the stretching and stimulation to even greater growth that new learning brings. When you feel stretched far and wide through pregnancy and new parenting, remind yourself and each other that this part of the journey is a physical stretching, an emotional reach, a mental challenge and an adventure you are taking together. Offer mutual support and humor.
- **Hope:** Feeling or anticipating good things or expecting the best reminds each of you that you are planning for your future while living today. You have problem-solving skills, goals for your growth, and solutions to any pregnancy problems that you anticipated. Have faith and confidence in your abilities.
- **Control** is the opposite of feeling helpless in the face of adversity. Control consists of feeling grounded or stable within yourself. Resilient people control what they can in their lives and do not worry about the rest. The real essence of feeling in control is that you feel you will be fine no matter how bad or intense everything else happens to be. Have you read the poem *If. . .* by Rudyard Kipling? Here is the first stanza, which represents the essence of feeling in control of life.

"If you can keep your head when all about you
Are losing theirs and blaming it on you,
If you can trust yourself when all men doubt you,
But make allowance for their doubting too;"

Resilience through Healthful Habits

Another way to build a resilience reserve is to lead a healthful lifestyle. Planning for good health and strengthening the immune system, which stressors wear down, means to develop health habits like good eating, an exercise program, and mental and spiritual fitness. What you develop now will be the legacy you give your children. So what kind of health attitudes and habits develop resilience?

Eating nutritious food is a priority in that you are feeding yourselves as well as your child. The basic problem with nutrition is that although we eat a lot of different kinds of foods, very little of it is nutritious. Nutritious foods supply nutrition; that is, enzymes, proteins, vitamins, and minerals that keep you healthy. Mostly these elements are found in live foods like fruits, vegetables and other plant-like foods. When we eat nutritious foods, we should feel energized and bright. Meats and dairy products supply our protein needs, and if taken in low quantities, our bodies can digest them without problems. Today, foods that are readily available for convenience and comfort drive most American food choices. These food preferences also drive the lifestyle-related illnesses of modern America such as diabetes, heart disease, metabolic syndrome X, allergies and asthma because of items like trans fats, hormone additives, preservatives, and more.

You absolutely must exercise, even if it is 20-minutes of walking or dancing per day. Bodies are designed to move. Think about it. Your heart beats, the lymph fluid flows, blood circulates, and muscles tense. Bowels move, skin sweats, and lungs breathe. Every vital part moves, expands, and contracts in some way. So, imagine that you sit all day in the office, and then walk to lunch and back, and then watch television and eat at the same time every evening. How can the body breathe, excrete poisons and circulate clean fluids and bloods if you never move?

Each day the average heart beats (expands and contracts) 100,000 times and pumps about 2,000 gallons of blood. If you are not moving, then your body is circulating toxic blood. If cells do not have nutrition or movement of fluids, they die. Make a healthy lifestyle choice for movement, any movement. Dancing, yoga, walking on the treadmill, lifting weights, deep breathing (yes, breath is an exercise), stretching with tubes, or performing Tai Chi or Qi Gong. Truly, there is a movement pattern, even for those confined to their homes, such as stretching limbs, rotating the neck or lifting the arms—all of which can be done while seated.

Breathing effectively and deeply restores your vital health. The human body becomes addicted to stress, just like it can become addicted to sugar, video games, alcohol, and other substances. If asked to take a deep breath, most people would sip in air through pursed lips, and then suck in the abdomen and pull all the air up into their chest and upper lungs. This is actually shallow breathing, which creates further stress on the body and produces the stress and anxiety hormone cortisol.

Deeper, effective breathing into the abdomen is one bona fide solution to the stress pandemic and is the exact opposite of sucking air into the lungs. Abdominal and diaphragmatic breathing are taught with certain yoga postures, but for most people, breath retraining is a necessary prerequisite to better health. Just like a pregnant woman takes Lamaze classes to learn a specific breathing technique to help with the delivery process for her child, you can learn deeper, effective breathing techniques that help with your general health.

Most people huff and puff in their rushing. They actually breathe too fast. Slower, deeper breathing, combined with the rhythmical pumping of the diaphragm, abdomen, and belly, helps turn on our parasympathetic nervous system which facilitates a gentle, but effective, relaxation response. Practice a few minutes daily breathing from your deep abdomen, fully expanding your lungs and relaxing. You will notice a positive difference!

Deeper, effective breathing expands vitality, lowers blood pressure, is used for pain management and encourages long-term health. When people breathe fully and deeply, the diaphragm moves farther down into the abdomen and our lungs are able to expand more completely into the chest cavity. This means that more oxygen is taken in and more carbon dioxide is released with each breath. That means relaxation.

Resilience for the Mind and Emotions

Music stimulates the relaxation response

Certain types of musical rhythms bring about a state of relaxed alertness and physical calm through an alpha brainwave pattern. Specific musical tempos will slow down heartbeats, lower blood pressure, and reduce stress hormones in the bloodstream. Don Campbell, in his book, *The Mozart Effect*, states that listening to half an hour of classical music produced the same effect as ten milligrams of Valium for hospitalized heart patients. Researchers have demonstrated that music activates pleasant feelings in the right frontal lobe regions.[1]

For that reason, music has emerged as part of the healing therapies and is currently used in hospital programs for cancer and other terminal illnesses, hospices, and in nurseries to stimulate infant relaxation and soothing. Some people even play music for their plants to encourage their growth.

Research has provided evidence that certain types of music alter brainwaves. *"Malyarenko and his coauthors played classical music one hour per day over six months to four-year-old children in a preschool setting . . . The classical music group had an increase in a part of the alpha rhythm (brain) frequency and greater coherence between different regions of the cerebral cortex, most pronounced in the frontal lobes. A particularly noteworthy aspect of this report is that the EEG changes occurred in a passive listening situation."*[2]

Greater coherence within brain regions produces a relaxation in the nervous system

This says that simply listening to music as a background filter can have positive effects on your body and mind. While most music researchers have used variations of classical music, research also indicates that whatever music you find most enjoyable will positively affect your mood. So use music to shift your focus, improve your attitude, and build your resilience reserve. Select from those that uplift you and make you feel happy.

Humor is an effective tool to build resilience

Most people have read or heard of Dr. Norman Cousin's book, *Anatomy of an Illness*, in which he tells his story of laughing his way back to health. Keeping a sense of humor during difficult situations is a common recommendation from stress management experts; so why not for those of us concerned with maintaining balance in our lives? Why do humor and laughter work? They are paradoxical to human thought. Just like music bypasses the mind and directly affects the nervous system, so humor takes one's focus off in a different direction.

Laughter and humor are so effective that one rising trend at the turn of the century are laughter clubs springing up globally, and they are a laughing matter as supported by research. Laughing produces healthy deep breathing too, so join in!

Researchers at the University of Maryland found that people with heart disease were 40% less likely to laugh in a variety of situations compared to people of the same age without heart disease. Did the disease cause them to stop laughing or is lack of laughter a symptom of the disease? You decide!

Researchers Berk and Tan at Loma Linda University School of Medicine have shown that laughter stimulates the immune system. Carefully controlled studies show that laughter lowers cortisol levels and increases the amount of activated T lymphocytes. There is also an increase in the number and activity of natural killer cells, and growth in number of T cells that have helper/suppresser receptors.

Resilience through Mental Fitness

Albert Ellis, PhD, is a renowned psychologist who developed a cognitive approach to understanding the relationship between events and feelings. Like other current researchers, Ellis was one of the first therapists to indicate that it is not events that upset us, but how we think about those events. Ellis' model to better understand emotions is called the ABC's of emotions.

- **A** refers to an **activator,** an event which triggers an emotional response or the adversity that a person may face. Let's use the example that a wife announces that she is pregnant.
- **B** refers to the **belief** about the activator. The wife believes that the husband will be as thrilled as she is and will have no doubts at all about moving ahead together into a new adventure. The husband's response is a warm smile, a "Wow!" and then silence. He is thrilled and scared because his thoughts say that this will be an overwhelming responsibility.
- **C** refers to the emotional **consequences.** The wife is disappointed that her husband hasn't gone overboard in joy. The husband stares at his wife quietly as a thousand thoughts run through his mind about how his life will change.

Albert Ellis believed that all persons have the ability to look at the information and the culture that shaped their beliefs, particularly those negative expectations and thoughts that keep people from achieving their goals and dreams. He also points out that all the time, people make inaccurate inferences about the information in their heads.

A simple conversation between the wife who announces that she is pregnant and her husband will clarify that he is thrilled, but also scared. In fact, she may assess her feelings accordingly and agree with him. They can easily stop their fearful thinking in that enlightened dinner moment and say, "We will anticipate any problems and plan accordingly. We are capable, confident, and competent. Let us remind each other of our belief and strengths."

In Ellis' model, step B for beliefs is the point of intervention. If beliefs cause the feelings we experience, then we should be able to shift our feelings by reframing our beliefs, thereby changing the consequences. Irrational beliefs cause self-defeating behaviors. Rational beliefs, supported by evidence, help us anticipate problems and solve them, and resolve any tension along the way. The way to change the irrational belief is to question those beliefs, find evidence or lack of evidence for them, and then dispute them in conversation. Often, stating your beliefs aloud or writing them on paper causes you to see and hear more clearly. Or you can follow Mark Twain's humor, "I'm an old man, and I've known a great many troubles, but most of them never happened."

Resilience through Visualization

Each of us has a remarkable ability to close our eyes and imagine another scene for our relaxation or create a different world for creativity and inspiration. With each picture we imagine, we create the smells, colors, flavors, and rich textures of the environment. Our sensory awareness triggers feelings of calm and quiet. Since every thought we have creates a feeling in our body, imagine the cascade of a refreshing, tropical waterfall drenching you, surrounded by the lush greenery of the rain forest.

Just as science has shown that thinking about running a race produces the same elation and bodily feelings as the physical act of running, then think what an activity, scene or creative endeavor that you take three minutes to visualize right now could do to enable relaxation within you?

When I was a child, I used to lie down on the grass to have the full expanse of blue sky and passing white clouds before me. This time was for catching my breath and daydreaming. I imagined that every cloud formed a different animal shape. People daydream to allow their minds a free-flow to places or spaces that bring feelings of joy, comfort, safety, and peace. Such imagery directs the mind and body to the optimal inner state for physical and emotional healing. Positive images specifically calm the nervous system, strengthen the immune system, and trigger healing activity.

Successful imagery has been shown to return a measure of control to cancer patients, enhancing their immune response to stress, and diminishing anxiety and fear about treatments. The same methods can enable us to have a relaxation response to stress within five minutes, just like taking a deep breath.

How to Get Started in Visualization

Before closing your eyes and creating relaxing images, find a quiet place to sit or lie down. To quiet a busy mind, it helps to practice a relaxation exercise like tensing different muscles in your body and then relaxing them or taking several slow, deep breaths into your abdomen.

If you are new to visualization, then start by remembering a happy event from your childhood or more recent memory. Your mind doesn't need to search for a memory or think hard about it. In fact, the approach is the exact opposite of thinking. After you have relaxed your body, just say to yourself, "I'd like to see some happy memories from childhood." Then stare straight ahead with your eyes closed, like you were waiting for the movie to start. Images will start to flow in eventually. Be patient and breathe deeply while watching the images. When they come, then you can get creative. Make the colors brighter by turning an imaginary dial to the right, "brighter" in your mind. What smells are vivid? Watch the scene unfold and fully allow yourself the happy and creative feelings that accompany the images.

Another way to get started for establishing positive coping responses is establishing a very optimistic, happy place that is personally meaningful to you. One skier always goes to the trails in his mind, and he practices his skiing during his visualization. How exhilarated do you think he is after his visualization session? Another client had a recurring dream of a shiny marble building that sat high on a cliff above the sea. It seemed to reflect the sun off of every surface. This ethereal-type feeling of the space brought her immediate relaxation as she walked barefoot on the cold marble floors through the building to a hallway with large marble columns that led to the sea. She would stand in the shade of the columns while watching the ocean.

Such a simple technique, which is not time consuming, can offer you relaxation in a few brief moments. Enjoy its benefits for helping you establish a resilience reserve.

Summary

In this chapter on building resilience, you learned that you can manage external stressors or stretch and cultivate internal resilience. The purpose of establishing a resilience reserve is to cultivate a "hardy" personality with a strong immune system that will not weaken when facing adversity or longer-term stressors.

Personality traits for resilience include optimism, humor, consistency, a sense of inner control and social support. Inner qualities that support resilience tend to be caring, compassion and the ability to take charge.

Preventive measures which enhance resilience are eating foods that provide nutrition, regular exercise to strengthen circulation and the immune system, listening to music and laughing whenever you can. Deeper effective breathing is also a single, important exercise which enables movement within your body of muscles, bowels, lymphatic and circulation systems as well as the lungs and diaphragm. Visualization offers the refreshing respite of going inside for awhile and closing out the external world.

Above all else, belief systems have proven to be the main determinant in our ability to manage stressors and have an inner strength called resilience. Irrational beliefs are limiting and cause us to have false expectations about other people and their reactions.

To examine and dispute our irrationality will keep you successful in moving ahead with your goals to be a new parent with confidence and competence.

Wallet Card

- I observe, assess, and plan.
- I am a resilient, confident mate.
- I eat nutritious food and exercise each day.
- I examine my beliefs, and challenge myself to truth.
- I practice a resilience-building exercise daily.

CHAPTER ELEVEN

The Sixth Secret

Trusting Your Intuition

CHAPTER OBJECTIVES

- Learn how to recognize your intuition and distinguish it from other forms of information.
- Understand what a powerful tool intuition is for making parenting decisions and life choices.
- Use your intuition to better understand your mate, your child, and yourself.
- Learn to trust your intuition, even above outside advice.
- Recognize your intuition as a wise counselor and daily guide.
- Quiet your mind and your entire self in order to pick up on your intuition.

The only real valuable thing is intuition.

—Albert Einstein

Intuition is the clear conception of the whole at once.

—Johann Kaspar Lavater

Mother's intuition. Sixth sense. Is intuition real? What does it have to do with parenting? Is any of it legitimate, or is it just a bunch of mumbo-jumbo? Before answering these questions, let's look at two scientific studies:

Chess Masters Rely On Intuition

In an article published in 2004 in the scientific journal *Psychological Science*, a Michigan State University researcher asserts that among chess masters, split-second **intuitions** make or break the master. The researcher, Bruce D. Burns, noted that chess players in fast-paced blitz matches have an average of 7.5 seconds to complete a move. Under these conditions, they don't have time to analyze in detail every possible move. Instead, they're driven to depend on their immediate **intuition**.

Both Heart and Brain Involved In Intuitive Information Processing

The California-based Institute of HeartMath, Inc., is dedicated to understanding and accessing the heart's intelligence. The organization regularly conducts scientific research on emotional physiology, heart-brain interactions, the human bio-field, **intuition**, and the impact of emotions on the body and mind. In one particular study, which the *Journal of Alternative and Complementary Medicine* reported in 2004, the institute examined physiological indicators of intuitive perception. Here's a summary of what they discovered:

> HeartMath researchers found that we can actually be aware of an event five to seven seconds before it happens. In the recent study, subjects were shown a series of images. Most of the images were peaceful and calming, such as landscapes, trees, and cute animals. Other photos, randomly dispersed in the succession, included violent, disturbing, and emotionally stimulating images such as a car crash, a bloody knife, or a snake about to strike. The subjects were monitored during the viewing for changes in respiration, skin conductance, EEG (brain waves), ECG (electrocardiogram), and heart rate variability. Participants' physiological indicators registered an emotional response five to seven seconds before an emotionally disturbing image would appear on the viewing screen.
>
> The main findings show that the heart receives and responds to **intuitive information** . . . This study opens the door to new understandings about intuition and suggests that **intuition** is a system-wide process involving at least both the heart and the brain working together to decode intuitive information.[1]

The first study shows that chess masters, often admired for their high intellect, regularly use intuition to help them win. The second study suggests that there is a biochemical mechanism which enables humans to be aware of events right before they appear, and that this mechanism involves our emotions, heart, and brain. It looks like the scientific community is starting to pay more attention to intuition, viewing it as a credible and even reliable way to obtain information.

This is good news for you as a new parent. Mother's and father's intuition is a real feeling that you can use to your advantage. From this point on, let's refer to it as parent's intuition. Tuning into your intuition on a regular basis can help you to:

- Make sound decisions for you and your family
- Understand your mate, your child, and yourself better
- Access information you may not receive otherwise
- Figure out which direction to go
- Find answers that will ultimately benefit your family

In this chapter you will learn to become more comfortable and more in tune with this important information-accessing tool called intuition. You will learn that often the very best advice comes directly from you. You will also learn how to calm yourself to help you differentiate between genuine intuition and anxiety-based thoughts.

Example: Putting Intuition into Practice

Alana's three-year-old daughter, Madison, is usually a happy, energetic, creative little girl. Like others her age, she can be prone to temper tantrums. Some of her outbursts are especially intense, escalating steadily in both noise and activity level. She cries harder, gets louder, kicks more and starts to throw stuffed animals into the air. Finally she falls asleep out of sheer exhaustion.

Friends and family offer this advice to Alana: Send Madison to her room, close the door behind her, and let her work the tantrum out of her system. Don't interfere. Soon enough, she'll learn that this is unacceptable behavior and she'll stop.

Alana listens and even gives this a try, but it doesn't feel right. Her intuition tells her that this is not the right approach for her daughter. Madison doesn't work the tantrum out of her system; on the contrary, it gets worse and worse, as if she doesn't know how to stop. Alana's intuition tells her that Madison doesn't have an "on/off" switch when it comes to tantrums. For her it's all or nothing and, left alone, she'll have a really tough time learning how to calm herself down.

Mom decides to listen to her parent's intuition instead of to the well-meaning advice from family and friends. The next time Madison gets into one of her hurricane-force outbursts, Alana lets it go for a couple of minutes, just to let her daughter release some of her pent-up anger and frustration. But then, she moves in. Very calmly, she wraps her arms firmly around Madison and simply holds her. At first the intense crying continues uninterrupted. Alana continues to hold her distraught daughter and starts to rock back and forth gently. Surrounded by her mother's protective arms, Madison begins to calm down a little. Alana keeps holding and rocking her daughter for the next five minutes, which is how long it takes Madison to bring herself from having an all-out tantrum to crying quietly.

Alana knew she had to provide her daughter with a sense of security before she'd even begin to calm down. She also knew that her own peaceful demeanor made Alana the perfect candidate for modeling calmness to Madison, who has a more dramatic personality and an intense relationship with life. She knew that it wasn't right to "let Madison work it out." She knew that she had to intervene. How did she know all this? She intuitively felt this to be the right approach for her daughter, and she chose to listen.

By the time Madison started kindergarten, her out-of-control tantrums were a thing of the past. Alana had found a solution. By trusting her intuition and using love, patience, and compassion, she solved the problem.

Some Truths about Intuition

Merriam-Webster's online dictionary defines intuition as:

1. quick and ready insight
2. **a.** immediate apprehension or cognition **b.** knowledge or conviction gained by intuition **c.** the power or faculty of attaining to direct knowledge or cognition without evident rational thought and inference

In other words, it's knowledge at your fingertips, a way of accessing relevant information. It's a sense of knowing what appears to come from nowhere in particular. In fact, the feedback comes from your internal feelings like gut-level hunches and prickly flutters at the back of your neck. Some people recognize this level of sensory feedback and others do not.

Throughout the ages people have relied on intuition to make breakthroughs. Scientists often use their intuition when trying to make sense of what they see in the lab, especially if it's new or unfamiliar. Einstein was perhaps the most open in his discussion of intuition. Doctors and psychologists use intuition, in part, when diagnosing patients. Creative people who write books and compose songs rely on intuition. Some people receive insight and creativity for artistic endeavors during deeply intuitive moments.

The fact is that everyone is intuitive at some level, whether or not we're aware of it. We may not know what to call it (sixth sense, inspiration, perception, or discernment) but we do use it on a regular basis. By becoming better aware of it, we can utilize it effectively in being a new parent and meeting our child's needs.

The point of the exercise on the facing page is for you to begin understanding the role of intuition in your life and your response to it. How tuned in are you to your intuition? How does your particular personality respond to insights you receive? Are you pleased with your answers? What would you like to change? Please make notes now in your journal so that you can incorporate any goals as you learn about intuition in this chapter.

Parenting Scenarios

As a person in relationships as well as a new parent, you'll run into countless scenarios, from the mundane to the urgent, where using your intuition can benefit you greatly. Here's a sampling of just some of the types of situations you may encounter:

Exercise: Are You Tapping Into Your Intuition?

Answer the following questions to the best of your ability:

1. When I get a "gut feeling" about a situation, I usually

A Ignore it and keep doing what I was doing
B Stop to analyze the situation
C Take immediate action
D Listen carefully to my "gut" before proceeding

2. I can think of at least one instance when I knew something but did not know how I knew it.

A Yes
B No

3. It's obvious to me when my intuition speaks to me.

A Yes
B No

4. If an authority figure gives me a piece of advice that I'm not comfortable with, I

A Accept without question what the authority figure advises
B Question the advice
C Go within myself to look for answers
D Ignore it and ask somebody else

5. Your mate walks into the room with a look of concern. You

A Get a sense that there's a problem and ask, "Is something wrong?"
B Don't notice
C Panic
D Tune in to try to figure things out

6. Have you ever thought about a particular person, and later that day you receive a call, email, or letter from that person?

A Yes
B No

7. Your intuition tells you that you need to take a break. You

A Acknowledge it, but keep doing what you're doing
B Listen to it, and take a break
C Chalk it up to wishful thinking
D Say to yourself, "Who has time for a break?"

1. Your baby is crying inconsolably. You've fed her, burped her, she has a clean diaper, she's not too hot or too cold, and she doesn't appear to be sick. You're rocking her in her cradle and singing softly, but it doesn't help. Your intuition says, *Pick her up and walk her slowly through the house while humming.* You try it, and pretty soon she calms down. She falls asleep.
2. You're feeling stressed and overworked. You know you need something, and you ask yourself what will help you feel better. Your intuition tells you, *Go for a walk.* You're feeling kind of lazy and you really don't want to, but you choose to listen to your intuition and take that walk anyway. On your way back home, you realize that you feel refreshed and re-energized. The walk turned out to be just what you needed.
3. Your mate comes home moody and tries to pick a fight with you. At first you're angry, but then your intuition says, *Back off; the fight's not about you. Say something loving.* At that moment, saying something loving is the LAST thing you want to do! You'd rather give your mate a piece of your mind. But you trust your intuition and choose to say, "Hey, something must have really upset you today, and I'm sorry you're hurting inside. Do you want to talk about it?" Chances are that is just what your mate needed to hear from you to calm down and release inner frustrations.
4. Your child is playing in the backyard with neighborhood friends while you're doing something in the house. Suddenly your intuition says, *Go to the backyard now!* Concerned, you rush to the back door and see that one child is hitting another. You hurry outside to stop the bullying and restore peace.
5. Your preschooler has been coughing, so you take him to the doctor. After checking your child thoroughly and doing a throat culture, the pediatrician finds nothing wrong. But since strep throat has been going around, he decides to give your son a prescription to antibiotics, just in case. On the drive back home, you wrestle with whether or not you should give him the antibiotics. You don't want your child to develop strep throat. At the same time, you

don't want to give him antibiotics unnecessarily, since it will kill the beneficial bacteria inside his body and probably cause diarrhea. Besides, you have no desire to medicate your child unnecessarily. In the end, your intuition says, *Wait and see. Don't give him the antibiotics yet.* A week later, the cough is gone. Your son never developed strep throat. The antibiotics were completely unnecessary.

Often, when you receive an intuitive insight you also get an indication of how urgent the message is. With some messages, it's clear you have to act immediately. With others, you have enough time to do some research, ask some questions, get a second opinion, or think about it. With practice, you'll get better at knowing how best to respond to your intuition.

As you learn to trust your intuition, remember that as with anything else in life, you may make a few mistakes. There will be times when your intuition tells you one thing, but you choose another option. Or you think your intuition leads you to a particular course of action, when in reality it wasn't your intuition leading you there at all. These mistakes may occur, especially in the early stages as you get used to working with your intuition. Accept this, and forgive yourself for not being a perfect parent, mate, or intuitive person! You're human, after all. With practice, you'll get much better at making good, sound choices based on your intuitive perceptions.

Example: Keeping a Child Safe

Steven wanted to find a fun extracurricular activity for his youngest child, eight-year-old Eric. His older kids were heavily into sports, but Eric was a quieter kid who preferred staying home playing with Legos, puzzles, and his dog. Steven did some research and found a local chess club for kids. He thought this might be perfect for his son, who enjoyed games and had a highly analytical mind. Dad became very excited—chess could well become Eric's "sport."

He located a website for this chess club and browsed through the pages. An international chess champion led the club, wow! Steven read about the chess master's previous experience, his many championship titles, and his teaching philosophy. He found out how much it cost, how often the club met, how old the kids were. Everything looked good; he was ready to sign Eric up.

But where did the club meet? Steven browsed the site further and discovered that the club met at the chess master's private residence. A red flag went up for Dad. He didn't know why, but he felt uncomfortable with that. He kept reading. The site said that the chess coach didn't allow parents at the club because they distracted the students, who needed to focus completely on the game. Another red flag went up. Suddenly Steven wasn't so sure anymore. Private home, no parents . . . his intuition said, loud and clear, *Don't sign Eric up*.

He was quite disappointed. Was he doing the right thing? After all, this could be a wonderful opportunity for his son, a chance to plug into an activity he might really enjoy. Maybe he was jumping to conclusions unnecessarily. But every time Steven thought about signing Eric up, the same message came up: *Don't sign him up*.

Finally, almost reluctantly, Steven chose to listen to his intuition. He decided he would teach Eric chess himself. He was no master, but he knew the basics. Soon an after-school chess club formed at Eric's school; parent volunteers were welcome. Eric signed up and by the end of the year he had become one of the best chess players in the club. Steven was happy to see his son bloom.

Two years later, Steven read a disturbing newspaper headline: International Chess Champion Accused of Sexual Molestation. He felt a sinking sensation as he read the story. It was about the chess master who ran the local club Steven had considered for Eric. He shuddered to think about what could have happened, and he was tremendously grateful to have listened to his intuition. Eight months later, the chess master was serving a prison term for molesting two boys. Both of them had been members of his "at-home" chess club.

When in Doubt . . .

Even though your intuition is a very powerful parenting tool, it's completely natural at times to question or even doubt what you receive via intuition. When you're in doubt, ask yourself these questions:

1. Does my intuition or impression come with a sense of authority, a feeling that this is true at a deep level?
2. Did I receive this piece of information as a clear insight, perhaps as a sudden burst of knowing?
3. As I analyze the situation and my options, does my "gut feeling" keep telling me basically the same thing?
4. Does my intuitive insight leave me with a strong sense of it being the right course or answer, even if it may seem illogical or impossible?
5. Does the message I receive intuitively feel like a solid, genuine piece of information instead of something my mind simply made up?

Answering "yes" to any or all of these questions tells you something: That even though your rational mind may doubt, this truly is your intuition talking to you. The more you recognize your intuition, the better you'll be able to trust it.

Coaching Tips to Help You Develop Intuition-Listening Skills

With regular practice, you'll be able to recognize and listen to your intuition better. By following these steps, you can coach yourself to become a more intuitive new parent.

Step 1: Clear Your Mind

Find a quiet moment during your busy day, perhaps early in the morning before others are awake or in the middle of the day while your baby's napping. Remove all distractions, including television and music (nature sounds, however, are fine). Turn the ringer off your phone, and let your answering machine or voice mail take incoming calls. Sit comfortably and close your eyes. Take several deep breaths, feeling your body, mind, and spirit grow calmer and calmer with every breath you take. Relax, and feel your mind clear.

Step 2: Pose a Question

While in your relaxed state, ask yourself a question. It could be about anything of your choosing: a possible course of action to take, an inquiry about a specific challenge, a request for a promising solution. Then leave it at that. Relax your mind again, focusing on nothing in particular by breathing deeply and slowly at a comfortable pace for you. Try to keep yourself in a positive, neutral place. Do not try to solve problems or force answers. Keep your mind open.

Step 3: Keep a Journal

Continue taking deep breaths. Take one more deep cleansing breath before opening your eyes and coming out of your pseudo-meditative state. Continue with your day, but keep your journal nearby. Anytime you receive an insight that you think pertains to your question, write it down.

Step 4: Review Your Journal Nightly

At the end of the day, right before going to bed, review your journal. What sorts of information did you receive throughout the day? How do you feel about them? Which ones ring true, make sense, or seem right? Ask your question again before turning off the light and going to sleep.

Step 5: Write Your First Impressions

When you wake up in the morning, write down your first impressions. Many of these will come directly from your intuition. Continue to add to your journal as you receive intuitive impressions throughout your day.

Step 6: Periodically Analyze Your Journal

After about a week, review the contents of your "intuition journal." If you've had the chance to apply the information you received intuitively, how did it work out? Did you find your intuition to be accurate? How quickly did the answers come to you? Are they starting to come a little faster now? With more authority? Continue to gauge your progress on a weekly basis.

By taking these six steps, you will coach yourself to pay better attention to your intuition, to recognize it more readily, and to receive answers more quickly with a greater degree of accuracy. The more you put your intuition into practice, the more you'll learn to trust it, and this will be very helpful as a new parent in learning to trust yourself and your judgment.

Example: What Does Baby Need?

Like many infants, Marissa's new baby, Kevin, cried often throughout each day and night. Having read dozens of books for new parents, and having listened to what experienced parents as well as doctors had to say on the matter, she realized that not everyone agreed on what to do with a crying baby. The camp was divided; some experts advised letting the baby cry, while others advised against it. Both offered valid reasons to back up their advice. What to do?

Marissa began to notice something: Whenever young Kevin cried, her breasts physically ached. She quickly realized, intuitively, that her own body was giving her the right answer: *Go to your baby.* For Marissa, it stopped mattering that she got conflicting advice from others. Her intuition told her, partly through her body, to pick up Kevin and feed him.

It wasn't long that Marissa learned that her husband Gene was experiencing an interesting phenomenon as well. Whenever Kevin cried, Gene broke out in a cold sweat. At first he didn't know why. But soon he intuitively figured out that his body was giving him the same message Marissa was receiving: *Go to your baby.* By listening to their bodies and their intuition, Mom and Dad realized that the right thing to do, in their particular case, was pick up their baby when he cried. Both of them were satisfied with this solution.

Take Care of Unfinished Business

You don't need to wait until your baby arrives to start paying attention to your intuition. Some new parents report that the nine months before the baby is born offer an excellent opportunity to "clean house," so to speak. It's a time to intuitively figure out what's left to do and to take care of unfinished business, particularly with other people.

Bringing a baby home is a life-changing event. To start this exciting new chapter of your life off in the best way possible, consider resolving any issues you may have with your mate, your parents or your in-laws. Listen to your intuition:

- What outstanding, unresolved issues might exist between you and your mate? You and your relatives?
- How do these unresolved issues make you feel?
- How might you feel if they were taken care of?
- What steps can you take to smooth the way to a better relationship with these loved ones?

By taking care of any unfinished business before baby arrives, you'll clear the way for a better support system for your family, more peace of mind for you and a better environment for your baby. Remember that if you have a mate, it will be advantageous for the two of you to build a partnership upon mutual trust, respect and affection so that you can parent as a winning team. And your parents and in-laws can be wonderfully supportive players on your team.

Example: Solving a Common Problem

It seemed to Anaya that the main reason her baby Serena cried so much was that she had a tummy ache. A few friends told her this probably wasn't the case, since Anaya was nursing and Serena was not yet eating solids. But Anaya kept getting the same answer intuitively: her baby was crying throughout the day because of an upset stomach.

Determined to help, she realized that what she was eating probably affected the makeup of her breast milk. Perhaps she was consuming some foods that were upsetting her baby's stomach. She began to make a list, trying to note when Serena cried more and what Anaya had eaten earlier that might have contributed to the increased crying.

In the end, she found the lists cumbersome and time-consuming. However she also found that when she made her lists, she was learning that she already knew the answer. So she tried something different: She asked herself, "Should I eat this?" before preparing a meal for herself. She then listened to her intuition. For some foods she got a clear Yes and for others a clear No, and for some the answer wasn't clear. But it was enough information to start making modifications to her diet.

She noticed an improvement in Serena; she seemed calmer and cried less throughout the day. They were making progress! Anaya continued to ask herself before each meal, "Should I eat this?" In time it became a subconscious habit. In this way, Anaya was able to intuitively decipher which foods were fine and which foods negatively affected her baby (via breast milk). By eliminating the offending foods, Anaya was able to prevent most of her baby's stomach discomfort.

Summary

In this chapter, you learned that you have a very powerful, readily available parenting tool at your disposal called intuition. You learned what it is and how to recognize it. You took an exercise to help you familiarize yourself with your own intuition. You read examples of parents who've used their intuition to solve or prevent problems, even when they receive conflicting outside "expert" advice. You learned how to quiet your mind and coach yourself to improve your intuitive skills, and how to handle doubts. And you learned how to let your intuition guide you towards any unfinished business that you and your mate need to take care of before your baby arrives.

Wallet Card

- Recognize those quiet intuitive moments where I receive clear, direct, and authoritative information.
- Allow my intuition to help me develop solutions for my family and me.
- To get an answer intuitively, I will quiet my mind, breathe deeply, and ask my question.
- Keeping an "intuition journal" will help me pay attention to and trust my intuition.

CHAPTER TWELVE

The Seventh Secret

Caring and Patience

CHAPTER OBJECTIVES

- View successful parenting as a process that requires a healthy reserve of both patience and caring.
- Realize that being patient means knowing that it takes time for everyone—you the parent, your mate, and your child—to learn.
- Appreciate the greater and longer-lasting rewards that come from being a patient, caring parent and mate.
- Learn the importance of caring for yourself, too.
- As a couple, learn how to coach each other with empathy and understanding to help one another consistently act as caring parents.
- Learn tips and exercises to help you grow in patience and caring.

The two most powerful warriors are patience and time.

—Leo Tolstoy

Whatever words we utter should be chosen with care
For people will hear them and be influenced by them for good or ill.

—Buddha

Rome wasn't built in a day, the saying goes. Neither do we teach our children and instill values in them in a single day. It takes lots of time and patience, and of course, caring. Since you have been working with a self-coaching model to be as successful as you can be in the roles you choose in life, these same tools help you learn to appreciate and embrace the qualities of patience and caring. You'll need to, because

- Your baby is going to make mistakes.
- You're going to make mistakes.
- Everything is new for your youngster as well as for yourself.
- What we adults take for granted, babies and children are just starting to learn.
- Being patient and caring with your child builds trust between the two of you.
- Building a trust-based relationship with your baby from day one will increase your chances of maintaining a trusting parent-child relationship down the road, even during the teen years and beyond.
- In the long run, your child will respond better to you if you exhibit patient and caring behavior.
- Patience and caring foster mutual respect.

Consider this example of two dads, each one with a ten-month-old son. Dad One believes that the way to teach his son to not touch something is to respond immediately by giving him a swat on the bottom. Dad Two has a different approach. He firmly says "no touch," gently picks up his son (despite his infant's vocal protests), holds him close while carrying him to another spot in the room, and offers him a different item to play with.

Even though Dad One's approach is swift and does get his baby to stop touching the forbidden item (because he's now preoccupied instead with his sore bottom and bruised ego), Dad Two's more patient, less reactive approach is probably better in the long run. Here's why:

1. Over time, Baby One may grow fearful or distrustful of his father while Baby Two will come to learn that trusting his father can be rewarding (as in being held close by Dad and getting a different toy to play with).
2. Baby One learns to respond to forceful physical cues, which is not always ideal. Meanwhile Baby Two learns to respond to subtler cues, such as his father's voice.
3. If both fathers continue to follow the behavioral patterns they've begun, Baby One will have a greater likelihood of rebelling against his father's heavy-handed approach when he's older, while Baby Two has a greater chance of understanding later in life that his father is just looking out for his wellbeing.

In this chapter you'll learn more about what it takes to be a patient, caring parent. You'll see that time truly is on your side, even in the most challenging circumstances. You'll do an exercise to gauge your patience level, and you'll learn tricks to help you remain calm and patient during stressful times. Just as importantly, you'll learn how you and your mate can cultivate patience and caring as a couple to create a stronger, healthier family unit.

Take a moment to complete the exercise on the following page.

Exercise: Are You A Patient Parent?

Answer the following questions honestly and candidly in your journal and jot down any related thoughts if they come up. This exercise is just for you, and is meant to help you figure out where you are on the "patience scale." In turn, this can help you devise a plan to develop greater patience in your everyday parenting, one step at a time. (In the multiple choice questions, feel free to choose one or more answers.)

1. In general, I view myself as a patient person. Y N

2. When I feel myself getting angry at my child, I usually
   - A Yell so my child knows I mean business
   - B Count to ten to calm down before speaking or acting
   - C Try to put myself in his/her place

3. To me, being a patient parent means:

4. On a scale of 1 to 10, with 1 being lowest and 10 being highest, my patience level with my child is usually a ____________.

5. When my child does something that makes me mad, I
   - A First react, and then think
   - B Say the first thing that comes to mind
   - C Think before I act
   - D Think about how my words will affect my child before I speak

6. One example of a time when I was patient with my child is

7. One example of a time when I wasn't patient with my child is

8. When I make the extra effort to be patient, I notice that my child:
   - A Responds to me better
   - B Acts up more
   - C Seems calmer and more cooperative
   - D Doesn't listen

9. When I react in anger, I notice that my child:
   - A Wants to get away from me
   - B Looks troubled or fearful
   - C Listens better
   - D Grows unusually quiet

10. To be a patient parent, I strive to create a harmonious environment for my family and minimize stress in my life. Y N

11. I'd like to be more patient, but I'm not sure how. Y N

12. In my eyes, a patient parent:
   - A Always remains calm in every situation
   - B Sometimes loses patience, but continues to strive to be patient
   - C Doesn't exist!

How did you do? Again, there are no scores. But through this exercise, perhaps you've learned more about where you currently are on the "patient scale" and where you'd like to be. As with anything in life, patience is a learned quality that takes practice to perfect. In the following sections, you'll learn techniques to help you become a more patient, caring parent. Incorporate them into your goals and action steps of your success plan.

Example: Trying a Different Approach

Linda had had enough. Even though she was a trained nurse, nothing had quite prepared her for being a parent to someone as lovable yet mischievous as her 18-month-old daughter, Annie. To Annie, everything was one big game. For example, every night at dinnertime she would crawl under the table and giggle loudly, trying to get away from her mom. After much effort and commotion, Linda would manage to catch her and place her in the high chair. Annie thought it was great fun, but Linda found the routine frustrating and tiring, especially after her long hours at the hospital.

One day, Linda decided the rules had to change. This dinnertime routine was no longer acceptable. She realized that, as the adult, she had the power to change the situation; after all, she had helped *create* the scenario. One way or another, she had let Annie get away with playing this "dinner game."

Linda's first step was to stop chasing after Annie when she went under the table. This required a little bit of discipline on her part. She had to learn to hold herself back instead of reacting or laughing.

Instead of chasing Annie, Linda decided to follow her *own* routine. She finished preparing and serving dinner, she announced that dinner was ready, and she sat down to eat. She didn't crawl under the table after Annie. She did give Annie a couple of chances to join her and her husband at the dinner table by saying, "Come have dinner with us, Annie." Her daughter simply giggled and stayed down there.

When Linda and her husband finished eating, both got up and began clearing the table. At this point Annie peeked out from under the table and started to get worried. They were taking her food away! "Dinner's over, sweetie. We're going to do dishes now." There were some tears from Annie, some hugs and explanations from Linda, and finally a compromise: Annie agreed to sit in her high chair and eat her dinner. Meanwhile the couple did the dishes.

The next day, Annie played the "crawl under the table" game again. This time, though, she emerged before dinner was over and joined her parents at the table. She got into her high chair without a fuss. Next day, she came out even earlier. By the end of the week, she'd stopped hiding under the table altogether. As soon as dinner was ready, Annie was ready to eat. Problem solved.

Linda never raised her voice, never scolded or shamed her daughter, never withheld love. She simply decided to stop playing the game and went on with her day. Patiently, she helped Annie learn about choices and consequences, naturally. Annie learned that she could choose to hide under the table, but then she'd miss having dinner with Mom and Dad. Or she could choose to join them for dinner and the meal would be more enjoyable. It took a bit of rethinking and patience on Mom's part, but it worked.

A Few Tricks for Tapping into Patience

It's easy to say, "Be more patient." The question is, how? Here are three "tricks" to help you access patience when you need it the most.

Trick #1: Give yourself a timeout.

When you find yourself running short on patience and perhaps getting too close to losing your cool, take a deep breath. Count from one to ten. As you're counting, feel yourself calm down. If you need to, leave the room while you count. This is a stalling technique. By giving yourself a "timeout," you're really "buying time," which gives you the opportunity to calm down so you won't act out in anger or frustration.

Trick #2: Talk to yourself.

Practice those wonderful positive affirmations that you work with in your personal plan. Hearing your own voice speaking to you is very powerful as a "stop and think" device. If you feel patience slipping away, speak up. Not to your child, but to *yourself.* You may even want to come up with a canned phrase (during a quiet moment when you're calm and relaxed) that you can pull up automatically when you need it. Your phrase can be anything of your choosing. Here are examples (feel free to personalize them to better suit you):

> "Remember the golden rule: Treat others the way you want to be treated."
>
> "My child (or mate) deserves my respect."
>
> "It's beneath me to blow my top."
>
> "I'll bite my tongue and be quiet right now."
>
> "What if my boss (or Mom, Dad, friend, person I admire most) were watching me right now?"
>
> "In the grand scheme of things, this is not a big deal."
>
> "Love comes first!"

The point is to get your attention quickly and redirect your focus. A slightly humorous phrase might be especially effective. One mother I recently spoke with uses this line on herself whenever she finds that she's getting mad at her child: "This is the future parent of your grandchild!" It forces her to think about a time and place beyond the immediate "here and now," changing her perspective immediately and enabling her to draw upon a greater reserve of patience.

Trick #3: Jog or jump in place.

Doing this gives you a physical release. Running short on patience affects your entire being—mind, body, and soul. Just like Dad Two distracted his son from a behavior, so you can distract yourself and change your focus. By jogging or jumping around, your body dissipates some of the anger or frustration that's building up inside. Think of it as releasing negative energy to make more room inside yourself for patience!

Coaching Tips for Couples to Grow in Patience and Caring

The good news is that you don't have to do it all alone; as a couple, you and your mate can cultivate caring together. You can help each other on a daily basis to grow in love and patience towards each other and your child. It's only natural that as you focus on being more caring in your relationship with each other, your baby will benefit, too.

Try these exercises with your mate. Not only will they help you grow in patience and caring, they will also help you grow in closeness:

Exercise 1

Hold each other lovingly. The more you feel love, the more it soothes your mind and energizes your soul, and the more love you'll have for your baby. Love centers and balances you. By holding each other, you and your mate create a safe, loving place for each other, giving you strength for your day-to-day parenting.

Exercise 2

Compliment each other daily. Give at least two compliments, one related specifically to parenting, and one highlighting a special quality you appreciate in your mate. Giving and receiving genuine praise will help you take greater pride in yourself and in your valuable work as a parent. Such a simple, respectful exercise becomes most important when you bring your child home and are busily engaged in baby-care. Don't forget to take care of yourself and your mate.

Exercise 3

Make a "patience and caring" agreement. Discuss what you both consider as healthy and unhealthy in your dealings with each other before the baby comes. Agree in advance to gently but firmly step forward when one of you observes the other in "unhealthy behavior" (for example, yelling, belittling, accusing). Agree in advance to listen to your mate when he or she tells you, "You're stepping over the line. Timeout."

Exercise 4

Brainstorm together. There are two of you; you don't need to figure everything out by yourself. Two heads are better than one. Talk together about a parenting challenge or concern you may be experiencing. Together, you and your mate can come up with ideas that may develop into solutions. In addition, you'll be supporting each other along the way.

Who's a Caring Parent, Anyway?

Caring parents love their children and want the best for them. This describes virtually every parent! But there's more yet to being a caring, loving, and nurturing parent. Here's a partial list:

- A caring parent understands that discipline means *teaching*, not punishing.
- A caring parent empathizes when the child feels sad, hurt, or lonely.
- A caring parent does not withhold love.
- A caring parent gives hugs and kisses freely.
- A caring parent uses kind words to encourage and uplift the child.
- A caring parent nourishes the child's body, mind, and soul.
- A caring parent takes time to laugh and play with the child.
- A caring parent protects the child.
- A caring parent strives to learn effective parenting skills.
- A caring parent creates a nurturing environment.
- A caring parent is warm and loving with the child.
- A caring parent is safe, approachable, and trusting.

Together with your mate, review this list. Discuss each item, pointing out how each of you is a caring person or parent. Use plenty of examples, such as, "I see you as a caring parent because you hold and hug our baby every chance you get!" Or you can say something like, "To me, you're a very caring person because you always try to cheer me up when I am sad."

If there are areas where you feel you both can improve upon, share these with each other. Do so in the most loving, uplifting way possible. You can never err on the side of kindness; your goal is not to blame, but to build a stronger relationship with each other. By standing by each other, and helping one another become more patient, caring parents, you will build a stronger family and a better relationship with your child. Isn't this worth it?

Example: Supporting Each Other Through a Challenging Time

Jason found his wife Ellen holding one-month-old Elijah in the nursery at one-forty in the morning, breastfeeding him while tears streamed down her face. He knew why: She was exhausted. Their son was up every one and a half to two hours, crying with hunger. He needed to eat constantly, around the clock. Ellen barely slept, her breasts were sore from constantly breastfeeding, and Jason felt helpless.

He had offered to feed Elijah formula, alternating with Ellen's breastfeeding. She wasn't comfortable with that, though; she felt very strongly that their baby would benefit from an exclusive diet of breast milk for the first several months. So together, the couple tried to come up with other ideas. They spent a lot of time holding each other for moral support. Jason gave Ellen lots of back rubs, and he often got up in the middle of the night just to sit with his wife while she fed their baby.

Finally, they decided they had to break some rules, for the time being. Even though others advised against it, they decided to temporarily move Elijah's crib into their room. Jason put the crib by his side of the bed. Whenever the baby woke up hungry, he reached inside, carefully picked up Elijah, and gently set him next to Ellen, who fed him. This way, she did not have to get up. When the feeding was done, Jason gently put Elijah back in his crib and sometimes Elijah fell asleep in Ellen's arms.

This new setup helped them get more rest; even though they were still waking up at night, they weren't *getting* up, and this made a huge difference. Feeling more rested, both Ellen and Jason felt less like zombies! Even the soreness in her breasts diminished somewhat.

As Elijah grew, he didn't need to be fed as frequently. The situation improved even more when he started on solids. By the time he was seven months old, he could sleep from about 11 PM to 5:30 AM without needing to eat. This was a huge improvement. The couple decided to move him back to his nursery at that point.

By being willing to work together and support each other during some very trying, tiring months, Jason and Ellen made the best of a challenging situation. Elijah is now a happy, rambunctious three-year-old, and those sleepless nights for Mom and Dad during his first several months are but a distant memory.

Ways to Care for Yourself so You Can Better Care for Baby

Taking care of a little baby is a big job. In order to do your job better, remember to take care of yourself. Here are some ways you can do this:

1. **Get rest.** As the previous example shows, this can be a challenge! Work together with your mate to come up with a system that allows both of you to maximize rest time.
2. **Pamper yourself.** You and your mate need to remember to do something just for yourselves from time to time. Take a bubble bath, for example, while your mate watches the baby. Later in the week, return the favor by taking care of your baby while your mate enjoys a long, relaxing bath.
3. **Accept help.** Your mom offers to watch your child for a couple of hours so that you can go for a refreshing walk. Your brother-in-law and his wife offer to take the baby out in the stroller while you take a nap. Or your neighbors offer to bring you dinners for a week so you can enjoy more time with your newborn. Don't be

shy—accept help from responsible, trusted friends and loved ones so you can get a much-needed break.

4. **Nourish your soul.** You can do this by listening to uplifting music, reading short inspirational stories or devotions, singing a favorite song, keeping a journal, or even doing a little impromptu dancing with your mate! There are countless more ways to nourish your soul. Discover them, and enjoy them.

Summary

In this chapter you read examples of parents who developed solutions based on patience and caring. You gauged yourself to see where you are on the "patience scale" and to determine where you'd like to be. You learned a few tricks to help you be more patient, and you learned that you are not expected to do it all alone. Your mate is there to help and support you along the way. You learned coaching tips that you and your mate can try to help both of you become more patient, caring mates and parents. You saw how nurturing your relationship with your mate could help in your relationship with your child. You were encouraged to recognize and appreciate your mate as the caring parent he or she is. And you learned ways to care for yourself so that you can better care for your loved ones.

Wallet Card

- I choose patience and caring as the better, long-term approaches to parenting.
- By developing a nurturing relationship with my mate, I can better care for my child.
- I am not alone; my mate and I can help each other to develop more patient, caring ways.
- I take care of myself so I can be there for the people I love.

CHAPTER THIRTEEN

The Eighth Secret

Flexibility: Going with the Flow

CHAPTER OBJECTIVES

- Learn what it means to be flexible in your parenting teamwork.
- Practice techniques to help you better "go with the flow" with your mate and your child.
- Understand the advantages of being a flexible parent.
- Replace the old paradigm of "strict vs. permissive" with the new paradigm of "clear but flexible."
- Know how to "pick your battles" in order to keep the peace.
- Maintain order and structure while being flexible.

Feelings of worth can flourish only in an atmosphere where individual differences are appreciated, mistakes are tolerated, communication is open, and rules are flexible—the kind of atmosphere that is found in a nurturing family.

—Virginia Satir

Stay committed to your decisions, but stay flexible in your approach.

—Tony Robbins

It's amazing how many different ways two people can find to perform the same task. Or how many varying viewpoints two individuals can hold regarding the same topic. You probably discovered this when you and your mate first decided to build a life together. Next add a *third* person into the mix like your new baby and watch in amazement just how many more ideas and viewpoints can materialize under one roof!

This is why flexibility is so important. First, you must be willing to be flexible with your own ideas. Next, you must be prepared to be flexible with your mate. And finally, the two of you together must agree to be flexible parents.

Think of flexibility as the ability to adapt to change according to circumstances. Yet, flexibility involves other qualities and concepts, including:

- The art of compromise
- The skill of diplomacy
- An ability to listen—really, really listen
- The ability to communicate effectively
- The ability to empathize with each other
- The realization that sometimes, right vs. wrong is not cast in stone

- A willingness to try new things in order to find a workable solution

By agreeing to be flexible, both in your relationship and in your parenting approach, you and your mate honor the unique qualities each of you brings to your growing family. You remain open-minded about possibilities, understanding that solutions can emerge when both of you are willing to try new approaches as necessary. Most importantly, by remaining flexible, you and your mate agree that fostering a healthy relationship between the two of you and also with your child is much more important than "being right."

In this chapter you'll learn more about what it means to be flexible. You'll see that you don't have to "give in" or "give up" on issues that really matter to you; you and your mate simply have to be willing to keep your minds and hearts open to exploring different possibilities. You'll come to understand the advantages of being a flexible parent, and that clarity and flexibility actually go hand in hand. Finally, you'll see that going with the flow helps keep the peace and leads to a family culture built around fairness and democracy.

You and Your Mate: A Flexible, United Team

As soon-to-be new parents, it is important that you and your mate come up with a parenting plan now. You've been building it as you've gone through growth skills, chapter by chapter. It's equally important that you both build flexibility into your plan. Take the following steps so that together, you can form a flexible, united team.

Step 1

Discuss your hopes and expectations for your relationship and for your child. By opening the doors of communications, you'll have fewer surprises down the road. You and your mate will know better what each of you expects. In addition, you'll be able to address possible problem spots well in advance, before they turn into bigger issues. Come up with hypothetical scenarios along with possible ways each of you might handle them. Always discuss your ideas in the most loving, open-minded manner. Try to reach a consensus that satisfies both of you. Remember, it's not about being right—it's about finding the best solutions for your relationship and your family.

Step 2

Develop a "What If" list together. Travel into the future for a moment and talk about circumstances or situations that might arise. The list from the chapter on problem solving is a helpful review at this point. What if our baby sleeps all day and stays up all night? What if our child turns out to be extremely picky about what he or she eats? What if we take turns reading bedtime stories to our child? What if we decide to take a longer leave of absence from work? What if we want to hire someone to help with the baby, or the yard, the house, the cooking? Discuss with one another what you'd like to do, or what you think you might do, in each case. Then, revisit each scenario and come up with new possibilities you haven't thought of yet. By doing this, you'll be better prepared to support one another as new challenges and opportunities develop down the road.

Step 3

Practice "going with the flow" to get a sense of what this feels like. It's a good idea to start now, because when your baby arrives, you'll be doing a lot of this! Here are some ideas for you and your mate to practice together "going with the flow" (just remember to keep it lighthearted and have fun).

- Leave one weekend completely unstructured. Don't plan ahead. When that weekend's here, see what kinds of impromptu activities you come up with together.
- Try something both of you never thought you'd be interested in—together sign up for a class neither of you considered before,

for example, or join a volunteer effort in your community. Going into something like this without too many preconceived notions offers you a fantastic opportunity to practice being flexible.

- Experiment with new foods. Go to a restaurant and try an item that neither of you has ever had before. Open up your cookbook and together whip up a new, exotic recipe. Feel free to add laughter as a key ingredient. Not only are you and your mate training yourselves to be more open-minded and flexible, you're also getting a taste of what your new baby will go through as she or he tries new foods!

Exercise: Do You and Your Mate Go with the Flow?

Here's an exercise you and your mate can do together to discover how well you both go with the flow. Answer the following questions in your journal, and whatever your replies may be, validate each other's answers. This is simply another wonderful opportunity for discovery and growth.

To me, going with the flow means

I feel that I am able to go with the flow
A Most of the time
B Some of the time
C Occasionally
D Never

A time that I remember being flexible is

A time that I remember my mate being flexible is

An instance that I remember when we as a couple had to be flexible was:

To me, the advantages of being flexible are

Some possible disadvantages of being flexible might be

In our roles as new parents, these are some of the scenarios where "going with the flow" may be advantageous:

Take as long as you both need to complete this exercise—a couple of days or a week. Give each question careful thought. Then, discuss ways you and your mate can help each other get more comfortable with "going with the flow."

Example: Going Out or Staying Home?

Erica and Samuel, an active couple, had many friends. Every weekend they loved going out to eat, going to the movies, going to concerts. When Erica became pregnant, they decided that they would work on maintaining their many friendships and continue with their active social schedule as much as possible after the baby was born.

When young Savannah arrived, their perspective changed. Many weekends they had no desire whatsoever to go out; they just wanted to stay home and spend quality family time together with their little girl. They still went out, but not nearly as much as they used to. Savannah fussed in noisy restaurants, and Erica and Samuel didn't want their baby to be over-stimulated by the loud sounds, bright colors, and hectic atmosphere that was characteristic of their favorite eating establishments.

They tried having their friends over, but that, too, didn't work out as well as they'd hoped. A few were boisterous and didn't know how to lower their voices while Savannah slept. Others smoked. In the past Samuel and Erica didn't mind, but now that there was a baby in the house, this party atmosphere was no longer acceptable to them.

The couple decided they no longer wanted to live up to their previous expectations. They realized that the dynamics had changed—*they'd* changed. With Savannah came new priorities, new preferences. They decided to give up on trying to schedule and structure every moment of their weekends. Come Friday, they'd just go with the flow. For the time being, they were perfectly content spending their evenings playing with their baby and then, after Savannah fell asleep, snuggling together on the couch watching a rented movie.

The Advantages of Being a Flexible Parent

Being flexible means, in part, being able to adjust to new circumstances. With a new baby come new circumstances, many of which you simply can't envision before your child arrives. This is part of why you need to be flexible parents. Once you begin life with your child, you'll be better able to tell what might work and what probably won't work.

Some babies do great going out to a restaurant with Mom and Dad; others don't. Some new parents are comfortable leaving their child with a sitter while they go out for the evening; others aren't. Many of these things you just won't know until life with baby becomes a reality. For this reason, being flexible is key to a smoother transition from being a couple to being a couple with a baby.

Of course, there are other advantages to being flexible. One has to do with which parenting style works best for children. There are parenting experts who loosely classify parents into three broad categories: authoritarian, flexible, and permissive. An authoritarian parent sets the rules and boundaries and stays pretty rigid with them. A flexible parent sets rules but is more flexible with them. A permissive parent sets few rules and boundaries. Each style has its advantages and disadvantages, but being a flexible parent seems to bring together the "best of both worlds."

The flexible parent does create rules and set boundaries, and this is important because structure is very necessary for a child. But if there's too much structure, the parent's role becomes something of a dictator, and the child does not get the much-needed opportunity to start making decisions for herself. The flexible parent allows for a measure of flexibility within the rules, which gives the child choices. The whole family operates more like a team. When you're a flexible parent, your child knows that she or he has a voice, and this is vital for your child's self-confidence, even very early in life.

Right from the start, even as a baby, your child seeks a measure of independence. You'll see this very early on. But your baby also needs security, structure and a routine. Again, as a flexible parent, you can offer the best of both worlds, allowing your child to grow, explore and discover within the appropriate boundaries you set.

A study conducted by the Boston University School of Medicine and reported in the June 2006 issue of the journal *Pediatrics* resulted in some very interesting observations. The study surveyed and observed mothers of four-year-olds from nearly 900 families across the United

States. Follow-up observations were conducted on the children, who were measured and weighed when they started kindergarten.

What the researchers found was that approximately 17% of the children of mothers characterized as authoritarian and nearly 10% of the children of mothers characterized as permissive were overweight. In contrast, less than 4% of the children of mothers in the flexible category were overweight. The researchers concluded that the flexible moms were able to give their children just the right balance between rules and freedom. For example, a flexible parent would insist that her child have a vegetable at dinner (rule), but would allow the child to choose the vegetable (freedom).

Coaching Tips to Help You Pick Your Battles, Keep the Peace

In the new parenting paradigm, too strict and too permissive are out, while clear and flexible are in. Doesn't this make sense intuitively? The question is, how do you achieve that happy compromise? Through practice, patience, practice, observation, adjustments and more practice.

You've heard it said before: Pick your battles. This is true in your relationship as a couple, and it's just as true in your relationship with your baby. There are some matters you need to be firm about, and there are other matters you need to just let go. These coaching tips will help you to better discern when to stand firm and when to let go.

Tip #1: Ask yourself, "Who am I doing this for, and why?"

We all come into marriages and parenthood with preconceived notions. When put to the test, we eventually decide which of these ideas are valid or practical and which ones aren't. When you find yourself having a certain expectation that either your mate disagrees with or your baby seems to defy, ask yourself why this expectation is important to you.

Also ask yourself, *who is this for*? If the reason behind your particular expectation directly involves the wellbeing of your mate and/or your baby, then it's probably valid. But if the reason merely is to placate Aunt Marge, to test a doctor's theory, or to prove your point, then you'll need to adjust your expectations, for the good of your family.

Tip #2: Watch your behavior, rules, and boundaries reflected off your mate or child.

Nobody lives in a vacuum. What you say and do, as well as what you leave unsaid and undone, affects those around you. Are you setting the right rules and boundaries, or are you being overly demanding? Are you setting enough rules, or are you being too permissive? Watching how your loved ones respond to you can help you gauge whether you need to become more or less flexible.

Tip #3: Pay attention to your intuition.

Your intuition will guide you as to what's important, what you need to fight for, what's trivial, and when to "drop it." Listen to your intuition. It will help you see whether you're being too strict, too permissive or just right.

Example: Learning To Relax

Barbara was used to doing everything by the book. A highly organized person, she needed every last item in its place in order to function at her best. Her mate, Gregg, operated on a more intuitive level. Overall he was a pretty relaxed person, and organization wasn't terribly high on his list of priorities.

When the couple had their first baby, André, their parenting styles too often clashed. Barbara, a perfectionist, wanted to get every single detail right. When she gave André his first bath, she had her favorite parenting book propped open to the "How to bathe your newborn" section and carefully followed the instructions step by step. Gregg found her method amusing and a little over the top; his way was to just pick up the baby and do what came naturally.

Little by little, resentment built up between the couple over their different parenting styles. Before they both exploded in frustration, though, they took a proactive step: They found a quiet moment when André was sleeping and they had a serious talk about their different styles. In the end, they agreed on three things:

They decided to give each other the freedom to continue with their individual parenting styles without passing judgment;

Barbara agreed to try to relax and trust her intuition more; and

Gregg agreed to, every so often, read sections from Barbara's parenting books.

By reading bits and pieces of the parenting books Barbara had read voraciously during her pregnancy, Gregg started to find more common ground with her in their conversations about André. By learning to relax more, Barbara started to enjoy her parenting role much, much more. And by allowing each other freedom, without judging, the couple actually began to learn from each other's parenting techniques. Friction lessened as Barbara's and Gregg's guard went down. Joyful laughter increased, and everyone—including André—benefited from a more peaceful atmosphere of cooperation.

Structure and Flexibility CAN Go Hand in Hand

As the previous example shows, structure and flexibility are NOT mutually exclusive. They can go hand in hand, quite successfully. As loving mates and caring parents, you can overcome differences in parenting styles to come up with a more cooperative way to raise your baby. Together you can develop certain rules and guidelines and a structure that defines boundaries, including a consistent bedtime routine, healthful meals, acceptable and unacceptable behavior from your child, and so on. At the same time, together you and your mate can help each other be flexible enough to adjust, adapt, bend and relax your rules when it's in the best interest of your child.

The road may be narrow and less defined between the extremes of "overly strict" and "overly permissive," but taking this narrow road leads to many rewards:

- A family with a team spirit
- A child who is not afraid to express himself or herself
- A child who feels safe, loved and secure
- A family that's able to adjust with the changes that inevitably come as the child grows in confidence and independence
- A peaceful, happy home environment
- A sense of fairness in your household
- Greater unity with your mate
- Better relationship with your child
- Greater peace of mind
- Less stress, more fun!

Summary

In this chapter, you learned what defines a flexible parent and why this parenting style, in most cases, is better than either an authoritarian or a permissive style. You saw examples of parents who adjusted their perceptions in order to find workable solutions. You learned that being flexible means listening, observing, making adjustments, and choosing your battles carefully. You learned that the point is not to "be right," but to make the right decisions for your child. You went through exercises with your mate to help you both learn how to go with the flow. And you learned about some of the rewards that can come from being a flexible parent.

Wallet Card

- With my mate, I will work towards becoming a flexible parent.

- Being flexible means we set rules, but we know when to bend or adjust them.
- As my baby reaches different stages, I will re-evaluate my priorities and expectations.
- I choose to go with the flow, for the good of our family.

CHAPTER FOURTEEN

Conclusion

In the Introduction of this book, I promised to guide you through 8 secrets that every new parent should know and hopefully master. I was spurred on by my clients and other parents who gave me such positive feedback that said, "New parents need these self-coaching tools to cultivate the characteristics and qualities for being a loving person in relationships as well as in parenting, even more so than discussions of diapers and discipline. The doors for respect, competence and success that open through self-coaching and learning about oneself are invaluable."

I could not have explained my desire to provide such a book any clearer. All the tools that you need to succeed are now in your hands, starting with the foundation of self-esteem upon which all success skills are built. You are truly prepared with new goals and actions steps in your success plan for clearer communication, problem solving and conflict resolution, stress management and building a resilience reserve. And do not forget your inner qualities of caring, patience, flexibility and intuition, all of which are necessary for loving and respectful relationships.

I want you to run with these empowering tools now! Reach for your dreams of being the best parent you desire to become. You have within you such immense resilience to achieve your goals and desires. And when you feel overwhelmed, remember the smaller, but equally important tools: take a deep breath, say, "I am safe and I can handle this," ask for help, daydream for a little while. Examine your beliefs when you feel stuck and open your mind to creativity. When you need a reminder, flip open this book and let it speak to your heart as it can serve as a daily inspiration to you.

I wish you luck on your journey, and I have thoroughly enjoyed being your guide.

Appendix

Wallet Cards

Below are the wallet cards you found at the end of each chapter. Cut out the cards and keep them with you to remind you of your goals.

- I have consistent, focused effort.
- I am my best cheerleader & motivator.
- I always follow through for success.
- I change one behavior at a time.

- I will focus on my goals and review my action steps of my personal success plan.
- I will make one change at a time, insuring I have effective results.
- I will read and repeat my positive affirmations daily.
- Emotional + Social + Spiritual Health = SUCCESS

- Don't be afraid to make change one step at a time.
- Trust my innovative mind.
- Repeat my positive affirmations, and modify them as life changes.
- Prioritize changes to be made.
- Look for ways to add adventure and innovation to my life, and then write down my goals to create innovation.

- I value challenges and failures as learning experiences.
- I set goals, follow them, review them, and update them.
- I communicate effectively.
- I keep a positive attitude.
- I am persistent in my endeavors.

- I trust my intuition.
- I communicate openly and listen attentively.
- I act with patience and nurture with care.
- I prepare myself through positivity for new parenting roles.

- I am accountable for my feelings.
- I stretch and grow beyond my comfort zone.
- I value myself and appreciate my mate.
- I practice self-esteem now to have healthy self-worth when my child arrives.

- I am mindful about what and how I speak.
- I deal with inappropriate behavior, not analyze.
- I balance criticism with praise.
- I act on fact, not opinion.

- Ask the proper questions and educate myself in anticipation of our pregnancy.
- Effective conflict resolution can lead to success.
- Remember the Rule of the Five P's: Proper Preparation Prevents Poor Performance.
- Creatively search with my mate for new solutions to old problems.

- I view stress as a challenger to help me learn.
- I am sensitive to my mate's needs.
- I will create a healthier lifestyle to support my new role as a parent.
- I will develop a resilience plan with my mate.

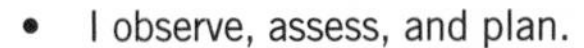

- I observe, assess, and plan.
- I am a resilient, confident mate.
- I eat nutritious food and exercise each day.
- I examine my beliefs, and challenge myself to truth.
- I practice a resilience-building exercise daily.

- Recognize those quiet intuitive moments where I receive clear, direct, and authoritative information.
- Allow my intuition to help me develop solutions for my family and me.
- To get an answer intuitively, I will quiet my mind, breathe deeply, and ask my question.
- Keeping an "intuition journal" will help me pay attention to and trust my intuition.

- I choose patience and caring as the better, long-term approaches to parenting.
- By developing a nurturing relationship with my mate, I can better care for my child.
- I am not alone; my mate and I can help each other to develop more patient, caring ways.
- I take care of myself so I can be there for the people I love.

- With my mate, I will work towards becoming a flexible parent.
- Being flexible means we set rules, but we know when to bend or adjust them.
- As my baby reaches different stages, I will re-evaluate my priorities and expectations.
- I choose to go with the flow, for the good of our family.

Notes

Chapter 6

1 Branden, N. (1986). "In Defense of Self." Memo to California Task Force on Self-Esteem. Sacramento, CA.

2 Branden, N. (1986). "In Defense of Self." Memo to California Task Force on Self-Esteem. Sacramento, CA.

Chapter 9

1 Stress: An in-depth report on the causes, diagnosis, treatment, and prevention of stress. Reviewed by Harvey Simon, MD. (10-10-2005) at www.well-connected.com/report.cgi/000031.htm

2 Loehr, James E. *Stress for Success.* (1997) New York: Random House: p. 149.

Chapter 10

1 Field, T. Martinez, A. et al. "Music Shifts Frontal EEG in Depressed Adolescents." *Adolescence,* (1988, Vol. 33,).

2 Malyare, T.N. et.al., Human Physiology (1996, Vol. 22, pages 76-81).

Chapter 11

1 www.heartmath.org/printer-friendly/print-ihm-press-coincidence.html

About the Author

Sharon Fried Buchalter, Ph.D., is a distinguished clinical psychologist, life coach, public speaker, hypnotherapist, marriage/family therapist, relationship expert, and author.

Dr. Sharon has a doctorate in clinical psychology from Columbia University and has advanced training in child and adolescent psychology. She has a successful private practice in Delray Beach, Florida. Dr. Sharon has developed revolutionary tools to help couples, parents, and families achieve happiness and success.

She has developed seminars and workshops based on her parenting techniques that are in high demand throughout the United States. Dr. Sharon has helped people from all walks of life, ranging from inner-city teenage parents to CEOs of major corporations. She has taught people all over the world how to increase happiness and success in both their personal and professional lives.

This is the second book in Dr. Sharon's series of self-help, parenting and relationship books. Her first book, *Children Are People Too*, has helped parents and children all over the world achieve family and personal success.

Dr. Sharon resides in Boca Raton, FL with her husband, David, and their two beautiful children, Daniel and Rachael. She considers her children to be her greatest success in life.

For more information about Dr. Sharon, please go to www.peopletoounlimited.com.